Japan's Direction, The World's Direction

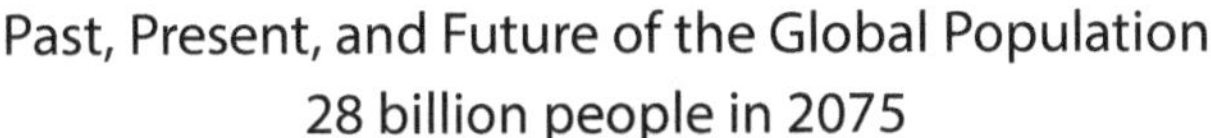

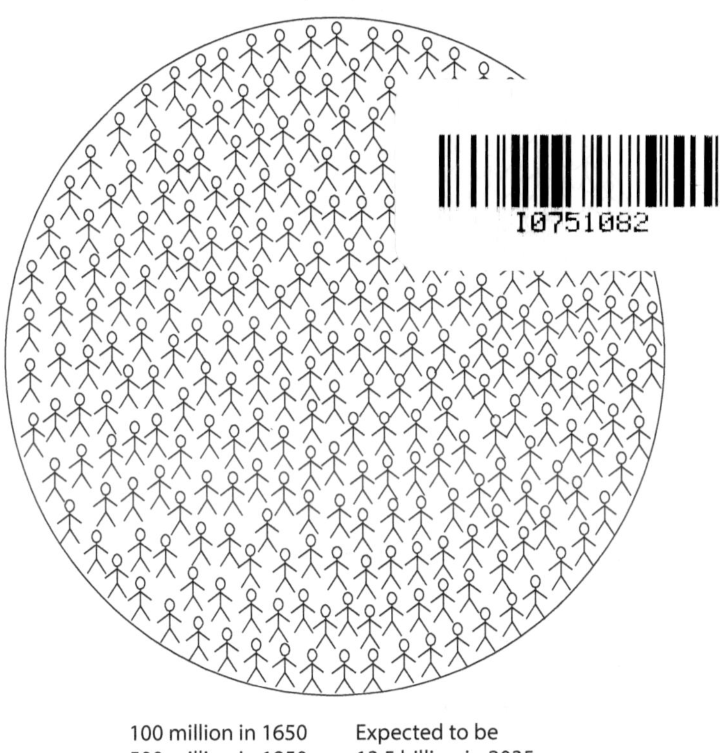

100 million in 1650
500 million in 1850
2 billion in 1930
4 billion in 1975
6 billion in 2000

Expected to be
13.5 billion in 2035
28 billion in 2075

ref. "Fate of Humans" by Morikatsu Inagaki

Tetsuro Sawada, Visionary Thinker

Japan's Direction, The World's Direction

Translator: Hidemi Uebayashi
Chief Editor: Lloyd T. Peace
Coordinator: Junko Rodriguez

Published by Babel Press U.S.A.

ISBN: 978-0991478989

Babel Corporation
1833 Kalakaua Avenue, Suite 208,
Honolulu, Hawaii 96815, US

On Issuing the New Version

Human history is very short; starting only 2 million years ago. However, when the human race set out on the path of civilization some 10,000 years ago, it immediately became an existence destined to live a life uncertain about the future, and even about the next day. On the other hand, wild animals that do not sow nor reap, can continue their existence on earth almost eternally.

Human beings civilized themselves with their brains. However, isn't there a crucial problem in the process of civilization with brains? I have addressed this problem to investigate the cause and set out the "prescription" in this book, for humans to stay on this earth eternally.

Humans are facing a variety of problems for the first time in their history. And that trend is increasing rapidly recently. Why is this happening? Believe it or not, my theory is that the problems are all caused by increased global population.

The world is moving generally in the way as I predicted in my book "Theory of Eternalization of Human Race" which I wrote 45 years ago, which explained my theory with a focus on the over-population issue.

While the earth has a limit, the population is booming explosively, causing endless desires of people, expansion of industrial production, mass automobile production, excessive speculative investing, limitless study tasks, disturbed human minds, economical competition, armament competition, ceaseless nationalism, and fights over resources. All these events appear to have no end, and humans will continue to expand their activities explosively as if the earth could grow larger to accommodate such activities.

This would soon let humans reach the limit of the tolerable range of the ecology of the earth after which the deluge will occur.

Why is this crisis happening at all? How can we climb out of it? I know the reason and the solution the crisis is happening because humans have barely used the other brain they have. If they develop and use it, they can immediately escape the crisis.

Humans have expended tremendous effort towards discovering and understanding various matters, but there are two key issues that they have not comprehended, or more significantly, they have not realized.

One issue is that they have not realized they have another brain.

The other is that they have not realized that this brain would allow them to see the logic that would help them understand every human problem in the society.

It seems as if no one has thought such a logic exists in human society therefore no one has ever tried to understand it. It actually exists as a logic anyone can understand. That's exactly the same as the flattening of the tip of egg in the story Columbus to silence his critics.

All phenomena occurring in the human society are, as a matter of course, caused because humans exist. Without humans, nothing would occur. This means that, in our modern complicated society where all problems are interconnected like tangled threads without proper order, once we give proper consideration to the existence of humans since their beginning following and the orders systematically, everything will become perfectly recognizable.

If we compare our modern human society to a tree, it is not equivalent to a young sapling, but it is more like an adult tree with dense leaves and branches. The body of a tree or the society represents humanity; this tree was born with the appearance of humans. Then it grew with population increasing, bearing branch and leaves as activity became more complicated, growing into a mature tree as it is today. Human history does not keep its mature form as a tree, but if it did, it would maintain a similar form as a tree that maintains the process of its developing history until it dies. A grown tree shows the process of the history and the present status of humans. Anyone can easily understand the systematic process of how a seed grows bearing branches into a completed tree. If we understand the process of human history that is similar to a tree with the other brain as we understand the growth history of a tree, we can recognize and explain everything clearly and solve all problems.

In modern times, the economic theories and ideas that have influenced the consciousness, actions, policies and economy of humans including the Japanese are "The Wealth of Nations" written by Adam Smith, "An Essay on the Principle of Population" by Thomas Robert Malthus, the economic theories of Max Weber, "Das Kapital" by Karl Marx, the Keynesian Economics, and the Market fundamentalism of Milton Friedman. Other proposals would be "The Limits to Growth" by the Club of Rome, warnings about environmental problems by Lester Russell Brown, warnings of global warming by former U.S. Vice President Al Gore and the IPCC, carbon emission trading suggested by Nicolas Stern, and warnings of human crisis by James Hansen of NASA, among others. However, none of them has not come up with the theories of how to lead the future generations. Therefore, humans do not know where they should head, directionless, as if they are stray sheep.

This new book "Japan's Direction, The World's Direction" is about a theory based on the philosophy gained by the other brain to precisely address this problem. Anyone who reads this book will clearly understand how the earth and humans are deeply interrelated and that all the problems in human society that have become too complicated and who is struggling to find answers, as if they have unraveled a tangled thread.

I have also described the problems of over population, food shortages, global warming, territorial conflicts, North Korea, wars, education, human minds, political economies, and disparities, as well as how humans should consider and behave in the future on earth.

I sincerely hope this book will be read by many people. I also hope that the theory expressed in this book will be applied widely in the disciplines of education, politics, policies, and others. For this purpose, I ask those of you, authorities in various fields, who agree with my theory, to write or talk about this book in various ways such as quoting the text or re-editing it in your own words for the future of Japan and the survival of humans. Since my initial efforts to spread my theory, the methods of sharing views of experts has changed dramatically, especially with the availability of digital tools to distribute opinions and feedback.

The power of the public is the strongest. If you support the theory, please spread it by word of mouth. If it spreads from one person to ten people, to a hundred, a thousand, ten thousand, to one hundred thousand, that will be the power to change Japan, the world, and the human race. My dearest readers, please give me your support.

Lastly, I would appreciate your comments either negative or positive or inquiries. Thank you very much.

August 1, 2021

Contents

What Motivated Me to Write This Book

As previously stated, I published a book "Theory of Eternalization of Human Race" in 1975, or 46 years ago, with 20,000 copies in Tokyo and distributed them for free to a wide range of people, groups, and organizations including all Diet members, all libraries, and foreign embassies in Japan, and additionally I sold them at bookstores across the country. As a result, I received positive feedback by mail from some 1,000 readers, both famous and unknown, who were as young as junior high school students to people in their 80s. I expected the book would change the world, but unfortunately, that did not happen. One of the reasons my theory did not change the world was that all ten publishing companies to which I sent my manuscript which I had prepared with deep devotion and purpose, all rejected it, saying, "We think the content is excellent, but even good books do not sell well if they are written by unknown writers. We need books that will sell well to keep our business. We will publish your book when you become famous. Please become a famous person soon," Following their capitalist business model. I had no other choice but publishing it at my own cost. I could not advertise it at all and could not spread my theory as I desired. Another reason was that the social environment at that time was not fully ready to appreciate the theory of my book. Besides, the mass media was not as competitive as they are now and did not cover my theory, leaving it unable to exert its power of change on society to date.

After forty-six years, times have drastically changed. In human society, populations have exploded, and also the desires, scientific technologies, economies, and myriad other aspects of human existence have exploded, changing the global environment greatly. Now the human race is in a panic as if it has opened Pandora's box. Even under such a time, as the social science (not as individual level but as overall level) that should have already appeared to be the brain for humans to lead them has not appeared yet, humans without an intelligent brain are practicing trial and error, natural science is spinning out of control, population is exploding, desires are growing infinitively, nationalism is flourishing, economies are focusing only on their growth, global warming is causing climate change, destroying the ecosystem and humans have a point of gridlock.

Politicians without a brain around the world are left in a state of confusion not knowing what to do under such circumstances. Scholars specializing in social studies remain as individual scholars and only acting as critics criticizing the politics and politicians. This is clearly preposterous. Having observed such situations, I shared the contents of my book "Theory of Eternalization of Human Race" which I wrote 46 years ago, about how humans should live, on my website and blog, made public lectures, and spoke when I ran for the House of Councilors election at the electrical district of Tokyo in July 2007. However, as I was still unknown in the public, the media did not cover me, and my book did not gain wide attention. Therefore, even at that stage, my theory did not achieve any popularity attention. This has allowed humans society to remain going out of control without appropriately controlled by the world politics. Now it has reached to the stage where we wonder the fate of humans.

Then I thought that it is waste of time to keep promoting my old book which I wrote 46 years ago. I decided that I need to publish a new book so wrote the modern version of "Theory of Eternalization of Human Race" after 46 years since the last version.

Names and Natures Agree

I have been writing this book mainly compiling the articles I had written on my website and blog. However, as I sometimes referred to my older book "Theory of Eternalization of Human Race", I was surprised to find that what I wrote 46 years ago is closer to perfection. Then, I thought, I should reuse best of my old book rather than writing a completely new book, as a new book would not beat the old one. Therefore, I decided to compile this book.

Several alternative titles for this book have come up to mind. As the saying goes "Names and Nature Agree", I thought these competitors will help you understand my theory, so I would like to list them here.

1. Clarifying the Relationship between the Earth and Humans from their Essence
2. Extreme Clarification of the Complicated Human Society
3. Why Did Humans Civilized, and Where Will They Go?
4. Past, Present, and Future of the Earth and Humans No One Has Ever Written About
5. Grand Design of the Earth and Humans (from the grand historical and overall view)
6. A Scenario of the Global State (from the principle of the earth's ecology and human society)
7. The Concept of the Global State (a concept only an amateur can come up with)
8. Great Development of Social Science will Save Humans
9. The Relationship among Philosophy, Social Science, and Politics

10. Human Suffering is Caused by Over-population and the Limit of the Earth
11. Global Increase of Population is the Cause of Human Extinction
12. How Humans Should Live
13. Spacecraft Named Earth and the Global State
14. Can Humans Survive?
15. Revolutionize Human Brain!
16. Human Fate Depends on Mass Media
17. The Universal Theory Human Society Should Follow
18. 5 or 10 Years are Too Late to be ready for the Crossroads of Human Fate
19. Miracle Human Brain Will Save Humans
20. Theory of Eternalization of Human Race II
21. Human Fate Depends on Brain
22. Constitution for the Human Race
23. Terror of Global Population Increase
24. Principles for Survival of Humans

Above are all of the alternative titles which express the contents of this book.

I have included the entire contents of "Theory of Eternalization of Human Race" which I published in 1975, so that you can read what it was about, and then I would like to add what I should say today.

"Theory of Eternalization of Human Race" (1975) Foreword

Today, the civilized society is not sure of its future or the past, or what is right or wrong, and has fallen in the vicious cycle. Some people say that human civilization may end in 50 to 100 years. There are many advocators raising alarms, but no one has provided any theory to stop the alarms or offer a viable solution. On the other hand, experts in politics say they no longer perceive the politics, economists the economy, futurologists the future, sociologists the sociology, and educators the education. Experts in all fields say they no longer perceive their own subject, making the public feel extremely anxious.

This is caused by sociology that has not developed at all essentially while social science has made great developments. It is obvious when we see the fact that everything we cannot perceive is mostly the problem of how to control politics, economies, the future, societies, education, human life, and natural science. Then, why hasn't social science developed? The answer is that the way philosophers and social scientists address social problems has been wrong. Social phenomena occur in relationship with the whole society, never independently. Therefore, to understand all social phenomena, we should first understand the whole society as one unit, then, under that perception, we should analyze or study each individual phenomenon.

Today's social scientists study society in a manner just like "blind men and an elephant". In other words, experts in each field of social studies do not share the unified perception of the whole society, but they study their specialized part of society based on their own values with natural scientific methods. This may help society be more complicated for them, but naturally they lose track of their specialized fields. I may have upset some philosophers and social scientists at the beginning of this book, but I strongly believe this is the truth. I hope they will be motivated. I have demonstrated the logics in detail in later chapters, so I will not explain here.

However, I would like to introduce the theme of this book briefly. If you think about humans as its original form beyond historical order, you can establish the logic that can see the society as one unit, and if you study society from this perception, you can understand social issues one after another. This view of general perception will be a great help as human intelligence, but if you further systemize the individual issues of social science under this unified logic and gain the unified and concrete wisdom, every problem can be solved. Then, if humans follow this wisdom, they can maintain their existence on the earth eternally. This is the theme of this book.

I am not a scholar but an amateur. I would like to explain briefly why a non-expert could arrive at this perceptive. Firstly, I did not reach this perspective by learning traditional systematic studies. If I had followed such studies, I would have never reached this perspective. I learned not only from academic studies but directly from history and nature. They are great teachers. Out of curiosity, I read about history and nature with my broad view to see through the essence which general people often overlook. I could achieve this perspective as a result. My not being an expert worked well after all. If I had been a professional, my study and living costs would have been covered by the organization I belonged to, but, I would not have been allowed to continue studying issues that the organization had no interest in. Many ancient philosophers were not experts, and that allowed them to devote themselves to thinking and studying freely. In the same context, I am not a professional and have done my own study, which allowed me to complete this book.

I have compiled hundreds of my shorter articles which I have written, little by little into this book. Therefore, many issues appear repeatedly, which I would like to ask you to excuse. I also ask you to understand that what I call primitive eras and civilized eras, experts call prehistoric eras and historic eras. Lastly, I would appreciate your feedback.

January 1975

Chapter 1. Thinking Life of 24 Years

1. Law of Development of Civilized Society

I developed liver trouble and was hospitalized from January to April of 1969 at Sendai Medical Center. During that time, I compiled some parts of my philosophical thoughts I had had since I was a student into a thesis and named it as "The Law of Development of Civilized Society". I sent it to various people representing their respective fields for their review and feedback.

Among the more than 100 people to whom I distributed it to all of the sitting cabinet members including former Prime Minister Sato, former Financial Minister Fukuda, chairmen of all parties, eminent scientists, critics, authors, the media, and embassies. About a dozen of them including Professor Shigeto Tsuru of Hitotsubashi University, Professor Masakuni Kitazawa of Toho Gakuen School of Music gave me their precious feedback. After six years, and devoting myself to thinking, and reflecting deeply on my writing, I found it somewhat immature and leaping too far, however, I still believe in my theory. For your information, I would like to share my essay, and like you to read it first.

+ + + + + + + +

I studied economics at Tohoku Gakuin University for four years from 1952 to 1956, during which I delved into the subject that captivated me when I was a high school student. I theorized that the desire for food and sex, the fundamental desires common to animals, was the primary reason for population grow in human society, and this growth of population is the driving force for human society to develop. Then, as I proceeded with this point of view, I understood all the processes of development of human society in the past, the present, and the future, and I thought that this way of viewing the world would be a great help for the progress of social science. I developed liver trouble and was hospitalized early in January at Sendai Medical Center. Stimulated by the article "Advocation of Desires" written by Professor Takeshi Umehara of Ritsumeikan University published in the January 14 issue of Yomiuri Shimbun newspaper, and also, since I had lots of time, to think and reflect, I decided to compile my thoughts into a thesis.

The modern time is described as an era of dehumanization or an era of loss of humanity, and many suggest that we are living in a civilization crisis. I think this is because the development of the natural science is too prolific and the materialistic and automatized civilization has accelerated, while the development of social science which is the science of the mind and the science for humans, has been delayed, making it unable to control the materialistic and automatized civilization. Therefore, I believe that we should speed up the development of social science and regain the power to control. Science, either natural or social, should start with understanding the most basic laws. To seek the basic law of social science, I started my thinking with the oldest human society, the lifestyle of primitive society. It shows characteristics such as 1) small and movable societies were scattered to places, 2) people in those times reacting to their instincts just like other animals, and their desires, intelligence, and emotions were simple, and 3) they ate natural plants and fruits, and hunted animals to live.

Observing these characteristics, I theorized that humans were not much different from other animals. However, they eventually left the animal society, fortunate or unfortunate, and built a great civilized society, which was caused by overpopulation and development of the brain. All animals have the fundamental desires for food and sex. Humans are not an exception. Humans in primitive times were thought to be living exposing their desires. However, the small difference they had from other animals was that they had the latent ability to think. In the instinctive lifestyle, when the desire for food was satisfied, the desire for sex was also satisfied, increasing the population. As the population grew, more food was needed. Gradually, limited amounts of natural food led to overpopulation. To solve this problem, the primitive humans started to divide their society like bees, and at the same time, they started widening the areas of collecting natural food or hunting, but gradually the territories of small groups of people came into contact with each other and they saw the limit of the expansion of the territories for food. Lack of food caused famine. As it was a matter of survival for the tribes, primitive humans were forced to make their latent ability of thinking work at its best. They applied the natural law to work on producing food.

That was how they started, but this ability to think led them to start cultivation and livestock farming, and that was what I believe the first step toward civilization. In other words, with this ability to think, a privilege given only to humans, they left the society of animals and stood at the initial stage of the modern, highly cultivated civilization. Therefore, I believe that we can say the primitive origin of modern studies and cultures began there. When food became available, population grew, and that required producing more food. Just like a seesaw game, economic growth and social development continued necessarily with no end. The human brain developed further as it was used more, and this brain created more food production, and also industries to satisfy diversified desires.

On the other hand, as society expanded, it contacted with other small societies due to the necessity of gaining land, bartering system, wars, gaining slaves, leading the society only expanding even larger. Naturally, the necessity of strong politics, strict legal systems, social order, and planning occurred. Furthermore, specialized knowledge in astronomy, agriculture, mathematics, science, among other fields, became required endlessly. Also, art culture developed to satisfy human emotions in prosperous life. All of these made the foundation of development, and the power to develop a civilized society, increasing the speed of its development. Once a civilized society grew out of a primitive society and caught the momentum of advancement, various changes occurred. They show respective principles which are easy to understand. I would like to divide them into three categories and explain each.

1) Change in Human Evolution

Firstly, as the development of society proceeded, various kinds of materials for living and food were produced, and cultures and arts occurred. At the same time, various kinds of desires occurred and diversified. Secondly, when society was simpler, laws, orders, and planning were relatively not strict, and humans were somewhat freer. However, as population grew and society developed, humans understood the necessity of having strict laws, orders, and planning. Humans in more civilized society have to live under the system with strong binding force. This is because a society with diversified people cannot operate effectively without strict force.

2) Change of Civilization

Firstly, when a civilized society develops out of necessity due to population growth, the speed of the development is accelerated while the quality is improved. Take the case of Japan, a civilization that has developed in 100 years since the Meiji era. It is said that it will be completed in about 50 years, which I totally agree with. In the future, I think a civilization that is supposed to be completed in 50 years will be completed even sooner, maybe in 20 years. This is because various accumulated elements of various civilized society will mutually influence on each other, becoming the power to develop the following civilized society enhancing it further. However, this acceleration should be slowed intentionally in due course. The speed of acceleration in modern times is getting too fast for humans to catch up with, but as it continues to speed up, various problems will occur not just in Japan but also in many countries around the world, inviting the worst crisis for the entire civilized society. Humans will be forced to conduct policies worldwide to redress the balance of civilization including restriction of population. However, if the policy takes effect, the development speed of civilized society will become like an empty lake drastically filled with heavy rain. It will be relaxed once it is satisfied, and people can once again follow the normal speed of development. Humans should take the control over the development speed of civilized society.

Secondly, as a civilized society develops, various fields are divided and specialized, gaining independence developing radially. This is needed for the development of a civilized society, and I think they should be developed. However, even the radial developments can be achieved, if they cannot be unified to contribute to human happiness, there is not much meaning. In the modern era, we have chosen the less meaningful pattern. I believe that is caused by the laziness of philosophers.

Here, I would like to state my own idea of the mission of philosophers. Philosophers should be the great leaders, using their brains to lead civilized society in any era. At least they were in the past, and I think that is the correct way. Modern philosophers have forgotten their original mission due to the complication of the society and act like critics. This does not mean philosophers gave their territory to scholars and have no further responsibilities. They need to realize that they have an even greater mission in the course of the development of the civilized society. Philosophy is supposed to be the foundation of all studies as methodology for them, and all studies should seek the truth with the methodology. Therefore, true philosophers should develop such methodologies to provide it as the basic foundation on which all studies are conducted. Furthermore, philosophers should supervise all studies to be conducted properly and work on making the study results helpful to human happiness. Philosophers should never forget that they have such a great mission arising along with the development of civilized society. Without philosophers who bear such a position, humans including politicians act with their tactile senses, opportunistic attitudes, and they have to search for the direction with a groping effort. The crisis of the modern civilization has come from this lack of great leaders. They have not realized their mission so far unfortunately because they have been unable to understand the law of development of civilized society as I have explained. It is more accurate to say that it was natural behavior, not neglect on their part.

3) Change of Society

Expansion of society continues from small entities to bigger ones with necessity until it becomes a single entity worldwide as long as population expands. The necessity for more growth as far as possible does not stop, therefore the policy of balance for civilized society based on population control should be taken. I believe that the policy should be made based on the elements of civilized societies that developed in the past. The future civilizations will have far more developed scientific technology than we can imagine, and all other fields will have developed as well in the same way, bringing all these elements into one planned society where humans can live forever. This means that the whole society will be like delicate machinery and harmonizing society into a most perfect system, which can be realized by the society that understands its fate, laws of the society and has a stable blueprint.

Stated above are some principles of civilized society and the process of development which I have found. I would like to explain some of them to assist you in your understanding.

In a primitive society on the earth that has a limit, once the population and food lack balance, or when overpopulation occurs, society seeks its people to use their mental ability out of necessity, and humans start to produce food. Then, unless it carries out a policy of balance in the course, a civilized society starts an indefinite development into a larger society until it grows into a worldwide society whether they like it or not. This is the basic principle of development of civilized society. The secondary principles would be diversity of desires, systematic socialization, acceleration of civilization, radially expanding specialization, among others, which interact with each other strengthening the necessity of respective development and the progress of the civilized society and accelerating the development, urging all to develop further.

Lastly, in conclusion, I would like to explain the meaning of this law. Because not just philosophers but anyone who has never found this law even though they should have, politicians have no other way than conducting politics with their tactile sense and opportunistic attitudes, like a boat that has lost its compass, and their citizens have been stray sheep. However, this will not the same in the future. As humans have found that the eternal law that is similar to natural science in human society, and by it, human society has developed out of necessity, in the future anyone will be able to observe human society objectively. They will be able to reflect on the errors human society made in the past, draw a blueprint of future human society, and confidently control the progress of civilized society towards an eternal existence.

This will place social science over natural science, control materialized and automated civilization, and also promise a restoration of humanity. When we look at the earth from a distance, following this law that can be considered as principle that leads to civilized society, we can picture it as the one observed from Apollo 8. We can also picture the past, present, and future of civilized society like a chart. However, even if we have discovered the law of civilized society, this does not mean that all the problems can be solved immediately. We have only found the law. To make it work, experts in various fields should understand, study, and apply it properly. I hope the whole world will start devoting themselves to studying it. I would be happy if what I have stated above will help people to correctly see the past, present, future of civilized society as a leading principle of it, and to judge if it is true or false, and also to solve small matters such as pollution and university problems as well larger matters such as contributing to building an eternal and ideal world state.

Lastly, I humbly ask you in wide range of field, for your feedback.

February 28, 1969
At Sendai Medical Center

Above is the essay I wrote while in the hospital six years ago. I would like to expand it to what I hope to emphasis as understandable as possible and consistently. Before that, I believe you will understand easier if I explain the process of my thinking that started when it occurred to me while I was in high school, and what motivated me to write this book. Therefore, I would like to write about them firstly.

2. Beginning of My Thinking and Its Process

It was in 1951, twenty-four years ago. I was a third-year student in high school, commuting to school 6 kilo meters away from my home in the town of Wakuya of Miyagi Prefecture by bicycle. One day on my way to school, one question which I still think is strange occurred to me. It was why stealing is wrong (not that I have ever been a thief), which was a grave philosophical proposition in a way. This subject soon captivated me and has even ruled over my life. That incident started me to ask questions to myself, which have not ended yet. The philosophy of Newton started when an apple fell from a tree, and my philosophy started with the question of stealing. I would like to share how my internal argument proceeded.

I did not think deeply about stealing as a human act at first but started with considering about stealing in the animal world. When I observe animals eating, I often see actions equivalent to stealing in the human world. For example, when you feed two cows standing side by side with two separate bowls, if the stronger cow finishes first and is not satisfied yet, you see it takes the food given to the weaker one. Similar actions can be seen among pigs, chickens, dogs, cats, etc. Not just among the same species, animals of different species show such actions. Not only that, but weaker animals also try to steal food boldly from stronger animals.

As I watch movies featuring wild animals on TV or other media, sometimes I see scenes where weaker animals steal food from stronger animals. For example, when a lion catches a deer and tries to eat it, some hyaenas notice the smell of deer blood, gather around the lion, and walk around waiting for a chance to steal the food. Realizing and getting mad, the lion drives the hyaenas away a little far. However, as the lion returns, a flock of vultures had already flown down from trees and began eating the deer meat. Getting even angrier, the lion jumps over the vultures which are trying to fly away, while the returning hyaenas are devouring the delicacy.

Considering cases like above, we can conclude that stealing is just a normal daily affair. Then, how about the early people in primitive times? It is unnatural to think that there was no stealing among them while most animals and modern people steal, and it is natural to think that they also stole. The items to steal might have been food sometimes, and hunting and collecting tools other times. To think this way, the act of stealing itself can be a habit of most animals including humans.

To answer the question whether this act of stealing is wrong or not, it is not essentially wrong because it is an act to comply with the natural law of survival of the fittest. What stops animals from stealing is not a feeling of guilt but the fear of resistance or counterattacks from the opponents. Primitive humans, our ancestors, must have been controlled by this kind of emotion to stop stealing. In other words, in the worlds of both animals and primitive humans, free stealing was not forgiven, but that was not by the consciousness of guilt. It is only civilized citizens that consider stealing is wrong and restrain themselves with their consciousness. This consciousness of guilt occurs from morality, legal rules, and systems, and it is particular to civilized citizens, as I answered to myself. However, questions came to my mind one after another, never stopping, as follows. Why do civilized citizens only have to establish legal system, regulate themselves, deny stealing which cannot be considered essentially wrong, and even crack down on those who steal? The most major characteristics of civilized society is a large population. When many people live in a small area without orders, as humans are animals with emotions, they feel pressures from each other, and it is difficult to keep good relationships and live in peace. Then, to make all residents live happily, establishing many rules or promises cannot be avoided. This is how countless legal laws and systems in modern society developed out of necessity of civilized society and punishing stealing as a crime is one of the actions to maintain the order of civilized society, as I answered to myself.

Around the time of that answer, my thinking shifted from the subject of stealing to the problems of civilization, population, and food, making it deeper and wider. These questions and answers were repeated only at the bottom of my consciousness until I graduated from high school, but after I entered university, I devoted myself further into thinking as if it is a symptom of a fever. I kept reading books in various fields one after another and debated with most professors. I was absorbed in studying my subjects during my four years of university life.

As I focused on population, some students called me a disciple of Malthus (even though I do not know his ideas deeply as I considered nature and history my teachers). How did the arguments develop after that? That is too long to describe here. Then, I would like to share what questions arose one after another, as I believe that will give you an idea what my thinking was like.

Why did humans shift from primitive society to such civilized society? Besides, it was only about 10,000 years ago in about 2 million years of human history, as if the idea hit them suddenly. Did they plan to do so because they desired to, or out of necessity for something? It is very unlikely that primitive humans desired to be civilized. Then, it must be out of necessity. What kind of necessity was there? Society is made of population. Was population related to the necessity? How did primitive people live at all? If the economic activities in primitive times were hunting and collecting food, did they have enough food? Was there a problem of overpopulation? However, if they had such a problem, how did it require the society to be civilized? In this way, questions arose one after another. I had to continue my guessing alone because there was no answer to these questions anywhere around the world. I further thought about what humans are, how they appeared, their relationship with nature, how nature and universe are connected, and what universe is, the questions anyone may have.

Then, finally, I realized that humans were civilized out of necessity by three elements such as population, food, and brain. I also realized that these elements can later became the motivating power of expansion of civilized society and its deadlock.

I think the four years of my university days from 1952 to 1956 were the time of no regret. Needless to say, my thinking in later years made my recognition deeper and wider. However, most of them are only an extension of the recognition I gained when I was in university. I have by chance completed my recognition of the foundation of the theory during my university days, that is consistent throughout my life, or the theory that is essential to make humans eternal existence. On the other hand, however, I did not study the subjects of my major very well.

I have traced back how my thought progressed briefly. I believe you now understand generally how I see and think. Also I suggest you read the section on what motivated me to write this book to understand further.

3. Resolution and Motivation to Write This Book

When I was a senior in university, the late Professor Tatsuo Nishimura of Faculty of Economics, who always showed interest in my study, invited me to his laboratory, and advised me to become a scholar to study further and present it. However, I declined that saying as follows.

"The theory I recognized can be called as law of development of civilized society, but it exists in civilized society, so I believe it can be called as truth, not a philosophy. Truth is something anyone can reach. Within twenty to thirty years, a specialist who studies society will recognize it. I hope to be an entrepreneur rather than a scholar. Therefore, I will leave this study to a scholar in that field."

After I graduated from university, I became an entrepreneur as I declared. It was in 1956. After that I quietly observed the move of society while living in the real society. There I observed the tendency that society moved faster year after year, and in proportion to the speed, everything diversified and became complicated. At the same time, I observed the phenomenon of increase of pollution, traffic accidents, destruction of nature, and isolation of humans. And I realized that they were caused by the great developments in scientific technology, and industrial economy were linked to each other without order, pushing up the society with impressive force. Under such social conditions, philosophers and social scientists who study society, did not advocate any theory that covers society as a whole. Therefore, politicians did not know how to understand and manage the society, always reacting after events. People's way of thinking became diverse, creating a vicious cycle. It was natural that citizen's and student movements occurred, making the society in uproar. Calls for true philosophy increased, but no one answered. What we saw was only optimistic future theories, eschatology, and alarming theories. Moreover, this tendency was seen not only in Japan but worldwide.

Even at this stage, no one reached the theory of civilized society as I had once expected that a specialized scholar would emerge in twenty or thirty years later. Anyway, I knew that the theory I realized was the only philosophy that would answer and satisfy the call. For that reason, I had been anxious watching the reality of society, but as I was too busy with my business and was not confident with my writing skill, I could not publish a book to share the theory. Then in January 1969, I was hospitalized at Sendai Medical Center and had a chance to write about a part of the theory and sent it to more than 100 people. That was the essay I mentioned earlier. Receiving valuable feedback from more than 10 people, I thought as follows.

"It is wrong that I am spending my energy running a company. As the mission of someone who knows the theory humans need most now, I should study further in earnest, write a book and publish it."

After that, and because I wanted time for study and writing, I stopped running the company and pursued what wanted to do. My thoughts and determination during that time are expressed in my greeting letter I wrote when dissolving my company. I would like to quote an excerpt from it. "... I made a philosophical discovery when I was in university. It can be a new metrology of social science. I believe that giving a birth to the new social science and developing it will not only correct the distortion of modern civilization and help it from the critical condition, but also make the greatest contribution to eternal peace and happiness of human race...."

Such background and determination motivated me to write this book. However, even with the determination, for someone like me who is not a professional author, the six years of writing has been extremely difficult. Even just developing my ideas on how to write for easy understanding while keeping the consistency among not just human society but also the ecological system of the earth and universe in a logical manner, took me several hundred days. Also, the unique content required me to obtain hints from various books and references, and it was hard to continue thinking alone. I had stiff shoulders and headaches and fell into a slump. My mental and physical abilities reached their limit several times. Seeing me in such a state, my wife often said to herself that I did not have to write this book since I am not even a scholar and wished someone else would publish this same or similar theory soon. What supported me to console and encourage her and also myself strongly. It has been my mental power, which has provided me with great hope and conviction.

Chapter 2. Ignorant Humans

1. Can Humans still call themselves the lord of creation?

People have highly praised each other for the highly developed state of civilized society as the achievement reached with the human brain and ability to recognize the greatness of humans. However, is that really true?

If humans have developed primitive society consciously with their brain and abilities to modern civilization, we can say humans are great. Even if they have not, if they understood the macro and unique principle that operates by itself in the civilized society at its foundation, and understand the civilized society correctly, and further, if they have operated the society to comply with the natural environment (ecological system), then we can say humans are great. However, even though humans have demonstrated their various abilities including using the brain, they have not realized the true relationship between nature and humans, and the unique laws of civilized society, or even where they are headed. As a result, and contrary to our opinions, various kinds of problems have occurred in modern times, and civilized society has come to a deadlock against our expectations.

Humans have never been great. On the contrary, humans in primitive times of nearly 10,000 years ago reached a deadlock and struggled through all difficulties to shift their society to a new civilized way of living which gave them a precious lesson. However, they have not taken the advantage of that lesson but facing difficulties at their deadlock they have reached again. Far from great, humans are ignorant and foolish beings. Humans were not born or live in this world with purpose or mission in any essential sense. They live supported by their instinct of desire to live once they are born without any reason. A life is all about how to live it, and this is the reason everyone has a desire to live it happier, live it freely, and to ensure that all of their desires are fulfilled. A society, a group of human beings, has naturally been controlled by such desires and ways of thinking, and in reality, a society that can allow its citizens to live that way has been aimed for. Politicians and most citizens have believed that this is the ideal, set it as a goal, and have been unitedly making efforts to achieve such a society.

However, in recent years, the awareness is increasing that these kinds of efforts were actually the efforts toward the destruction of humans. This is a fearful, inconsistent argument that cannot happen. However, this is the truth. Humans have been marching toward its death without knowing it. The speed of development is fast; unless the direction of the efforts is changed immediately, humans will reach the wrong goal, not the real goal. They are making great efforts to bring happiness to themselves, but those were the efforts to destroy themselves in the end as if it is a horror story. I was shocked to know that that this result has been caused 100% from ignorance and stupidity of humans. Not realizing their own ignorance and still calling themselves the lord of creation; how stupid humans are.

Humans have created a kind of fortress called society in the natural world with their brain. They should have been aware of this true relationship between nature and humans, between society and humans, and choose a forever accurate and balanced way of life among nature, society, and humans. In other words, as they say, "Know your enemy, know thyself, and you shall not fear a hundred battles", even if it is not about war, humans should have acquired the knowledge about nature, society, and humans, and lived a balanced life that would never cause a deviation. However, humans have not been good at seeing the essence of things or seeing with a broad perspective. They have never understood nature, society, and humans from such a point of view. Therefore, not only did they learn the true relationship among the three parties, but they also did not learn the existence of the important principle for civilized society. They have just given them their own explanation on what nature is, what society is, and what the relationship among the three parties is. Despite the fact that there has been a distance or space between human consciousness and nature or society, they have failed to realize this fact, and they have just made a close connection with society blindly. Therefore, let alone achieving goals, it is getting difficult for humans to survive any further due to the logic of nature and society.

Needless to say, all these events are, of course, caused by ignorance and stupidity of humans. Nature and society never run or hide away. Because it is humans who are supposed to understand that do not understand or follow up, tragedies or destruction are about to happen. Therefore, it is well-earned punishment for humans themselves.

However, nature and society that stand neutral do not wish that to happen. They do not deny either humans to grow wiser to keep a good balance with nature and operate society. Humans should know that of the three parties of nature, society and humans, the problem is always with humans.

2. Humans Create Inconsistency Themselves

Rumors say that humans might be extinct in 50 to 100 years. Indeed, there is no material evidence to have an optimistic view. Extinction would not be caused by the change of nature itself but by the actions caused by humans ignorance. There are various laws in nature; if we learn them, we can use or apply nature freely. It is a theory that, however, if we become overconfident and keep using or applying nature, that will change the earth's environment to the stage where humans cannot live anymore, and as a result, humans will be forced to become extinct.

Since the beginning of civilization, because they are a little clever, humans have been conceited and considered that they were created to be similar to God, that they created civilization, or that they are the lords of creation, and have looked down on other animals. However, the animals that are supposed to be wild and ignorant have potential to survive 100 years or forever if they escape from being involved with human extinction, while humans are facing the danger of extinction in 50 or 100 years. Civilized citizens who live with their brain are the losers when we talk about the ability to survive. Even if they say longevity alone is not everything, if they flourish and become extinct in 10,000 years, that is only the howl of the losing dog. This attribute to the problem of humans with living a life using the brain, but this is a great inconsistency to the conception of humans. Humans could create civilization because they have good brains, and when ignorant animals go extinct, we humans could keep its existence forever, which is totally opposite to our existing conventions.

Why does such inconsistency occur only in humans, and why do only humans have to face the crisis of extinction? That is because the crisis is caused not by nature but by humans that have problems. The crisis is not a natural disaster but a human disaster. It is that the crisis occurs because the human brain is incomplete. (I will explain this later.). However, it is fortunate that these inconsistencies and crisis are occurring by the incompletion of humans, because if humans are well prepared, they can overcome them. They can even exist forever.

I would like to explain this in detail.

If humans polish their brain and completely comply with the logic of nature, they can remain on earth for billions of years to come. The grounds of this theory are the fact that the earth has existed for 45 billion years, and it is thought that it will remain the same 45 billion years to come. If that is so, living organisms can exist for about 30 billion years or more, and during that time, humans should be able to exist for a few billion years.

To explain more concretely, the earth will go extinct in about 45 billion years because the sun will grow into a bigger planet and engulf the earth. Then naturally, the closer the sun that has become enormous gets to the earth, the faster the earth degrades its environment for living organisms, but as this will happen in the remote future, the earth will keep its environment available for humans to live for a few billions of years. Of course, this is on the condition that humans as one of the living organisms on earth will develop themselves (including development by civilized means) complying with the change of nature. It is certain that the earth will accommodate humans if they try to adapt themselves properly for an unimaginably long time.

3. Humans Think Based on Society Only

Today, most people around the world live in civilized society that is a kind of fortress against nature. If we think about the ways of thinking and topics occurring there, humans have sought everything within the civilized society that is formed while blocking off history and nature, like the frog in the well. We can try to apply reasons to each problem of politics, economy, education, and culture, that are interconnected like a tangled thread in civilized society. However, we can hardly recognize or reason the entire scope of the problems objectively or consistently.

While everything stands objectively, why can't we give them an objective and consistent explanation? This is because most people are the frogs in the well, making their minds and ideology go in a negative cycle in the fortress-like civilized society. To have the consciousness that can see things consistently and that can predict the future, we should grow out of the attitude of understanding everything in civilized society to shift to the historical view that sees civilized society as the modified version of primitive times. And at the same time, we should change to a highly broad view to comply with nature that is the foundation or vessel of civilized society.

Not only Arnold Toynbee, an historian and also philosopher, most intellects in various fields around the world have ignored the primitive life of humans that lasted as long as about 2 million years, and see the civilized and modern life that has existed only less than 10,000 years as the genuine life of humans. Furthermore, they seek tips for a better life only to the history of after civilization, other animals, and operation systems of other countries. They do not try learning from the long history of life before civilization consistently. Here lies the mistake. Modern humans are the result of an extremely long history. Without following this fact, we can never have the correct ideology nor the lifestyle. If we do not see a tree from the root or trunk but only branches and leaves, our ideology will go into the negative cycle never finding the root or trunk. The lifestyle based only on such ideology will naturally be the lifestyle that will never comply with the logic of nature.

Human history is said to be about 2 million years, of which, except about 10,000 years after civilization, 1.99 million years, or 99.5%, was primitive times for humans. Today, most people see the long time before civilization as an animal, wild or abnormal way of life, and on the other hand, see the 10,000 years, or short civilization time, or 0.5% of all history, as humans, civilized, or normal way of life. Why do they only see or think within the frame of the short history of small, civilized society? Why do they seek meaning of everything within the frame of the short history of small, civilized society like the frog in the well? This is the reason why we cannot see anything.

Humans have seen the history of life of more than 30 million years and 1.99 million years of history of humans before civilization equally, and probably for that reason they have left the study of them to archaeologists and biologists. There was no initiative to study the whole history to find the proper way of human life after civilization. It is as if humans have become a new species after civilization and it is no use studying about the history before that and cut off the primitive history in order to study matters within civilization. Therefore, no one has asked or answered the question of why humans had to shift their lifestyle to civilization after about 1,990,000 years since its beginning.

When we see the living way of humans after civilization in the light of about 2 million years of human history, it is a totally special, abnormal way. Seeing it not consecutively caused humans to realize that, and further caused humans to believe it is the true way of human life. Even observing the complicated society totally on the same dimension, you cannot understand the fundamental universal essence, nor the present and future. The present times are the consequence of the long history. You cannot understand the modern society without focusing on the essence in the context of the long history.

4. Priorities Misplaced

Civilized society is adding more speed to its complexity day by day. Besides, it creates various kinds of pollution without showing where it is heading. Humans, who are supposed to bear the leading role of society, are buried in such society, and dragged by the society which is a preposterous situation. Such a relationship between humans and society has existed only less than 10,000 years since civilization, not for 2 million years since the beginning of humans. In primitive times, such priority reversed relationship did not occur or could not occur. This is because in those times the society was a simple group of people, different from today's society in its quality. Society itself did not have ability of self-operation, and humans led their lives directly adapting themselves to nature not like today.

Humans, who were originally wild beings, were civilized due to the overpopulation on earth that has a limit and also due to the evolution of the brain. In other words, population growth exceeded the natural food provided on earth with finite limit, bringing about the problem of overpopulation reaching the limit and food shortage, but at that time humans already had their brain evolved, and with that they developed agriculture and farming, and shifted to a new lifestyle, a civilized lifestyle. Humans should be aware of this fact to avoid making the same mistake and live wisely.

However, the people who lived at the beginning of civilized times worked hard thinking only to shift their deadlocked life to a freer lifestyle. They did not have the room or necessity to think that way. For this reason, humans who lived in the first society (primitive lifestyle of 1.99 million years) did not break up with their old lifestyle to start the second lifestyle (lifestyle since the beginning of civilization to the third lifestyle), but they shifted to the second lifestyle maintaining the old ideology mainly on their instinct. Therefore, the second lifestyle is the extension of the first lifestyle. Civilized people lived a civilized lifestyle in form, but actually it was primitive based on instincts and with old ideas.

This corresponds to the incomplete state of the brain which I will explain later. On the extension of this incomplete state and the first lifestyle, only scientific cognition displayed its ability and created today's civilization. To explain this in the opposite way, as the other ability of philosophical cognition that judges things totally or control of the civilization remains undisplayed, civilization is operating itself to be the modern state. This tendency started at the beginning of civilization, so people see that as natural. Therefore, humans have affirmed the reality unconditionally, and adjusted themselves to that while burying themselves. Here occurs the discrepancy between the truth and the reality, causing the situation where priorities are misplaced.

Originally, the human brain is dual structured. Humans have not been good at seeing things highly essentially and broadly, or philosophically. In addition to this fact, due to the reality that they had survived with their ability of scientific cognition, the ability of philosophical cognition has not had a chance to appear. However, this philosophical cognition should have appeared and worked in balance with the scientific cognition. As it has been undisplayed remaining not in action, civilized society has become priorities misplaced society without noticing that. There would be no big problem if humans can continue leading the current lifestyle, but this situation cannot be continued any longer. We should have the philosophical cognitive ability displaced and let it normalize the civilized priorities in a misplaced society, save humans from extinction, and let it remain eternally.

This is also the theme of this book.

5. Vicious Cycle of Thinking

One of today's serious problems is traffic. Cars are mass produced endlessly at factories, and most of them are being driven in cities. Even though some are balanced out by replacements, the actual number is only increasing. Every street is full of cars. Even as new roads are built, new traffic rules are made, and more crossing guards are deployed, traffic conditions are only getting worse day by day. Most drivers must drive and are repeatedly experiencing irritation every day. When there are more cars on the street than a certain density, drivers have more difficulties. I feel the same as I drive. I wonder what will happen in 10 years, or later in the future? Even with today's tense traffic situation, we do not hear that politicians and scholars have solved the traffic problems drastically, nor have they announced their vision or are preparing to never allow any traffic problems in the future. Is it impossible that the modern brain is lacking the total planning ability that can produce any drastic plan to address traffic problems? If they cannot, then they have no other choice than carrying out countermeasures in a whack-a-mole way until it is not effective anymore. As a result, it will see a deadlock sometime in the future, and force them to make a changeover like the time of the agricultural policy, that is the shift from encouraging rice production to an acreage-reduction policy, or even more drastic change.

However, even in such times, quite a few of those who are engaged in cult religions or who do not see things deeply consider the reality where there are many cars on the streets, roads are established to catch up with the traffic, new traffic laws are enforced, crossing guards are standing along the streets, making roads complicated, is progress. They believe in an optimistic way that humans have wisdom with which they can solve traffic problems whenever they occur. This traffic problem is only one phenomenon in civilized society. In civilized society, there are countless problems such as population, pollution, and land, just like traffic problems. Then, how about the civilized society encompassing all of them? It is just the larger version of such problems. Rather, should we say that because the overall civilized society is making a vicious cycle, individual phenomenon is happening as such.

The monster called civil society has diversified beyond our understanding and ability to respond. It is heading into its own direction at its full speed without concerning the direction we hope for. The fact that we cannot understand society means not just that we cannot control society as we wish, but also that it is getting more difficult to adapt ourselves to society. It sounds inconsistent that we do not understand the society we live in. However, if this situation continues, there will be no other way for humans and society destroy will ourselves. Our fate is that we will not be saved unless a totally new truth or philosophy appear to solve all the problems altogether.

Today, many social scientists and thinkers often say that the situation cannot change unless a new and affirmative methodology is developed. Here is a little old example. From April 10, 1970, International Future Conference was held at Kyoto International Conference Center for one week attended by 271 futurologists from 33 countries including Japan. During the event, under the unified theme of "Challenges from the Future", they discussed issues of methodology of futurology, sense of values, and global future problems. However, even though they discussed future society when social science itself was only in name, it was only natural they did not reach good conclusions, and it looked like the discussions were empty. Social science that was supposed to be the foundation was like sand. It was natural that discussions about future society ended up like a castle in the air. Some of the participants realized that and mentioned that the development of true methodology was the priority, and that without the theory it was difficult to discuss future society, and make social science progress further.

Most people so far have accepted the existing society as it is, and see and think about things in the framework of society, their ideas are piddling details, seeking, and widely diversified. Even the idea that looks deep does not see beyond itself, making it a vicious cycle as the idea for the whole society. Under the current social situation, mass media flourishes, and information floods. While drawing in it, people struggle for the truth, but what they reach are mostly scallion skins and do not give us any vital power. People in society are straying more and losing direction.

To explain briefly, science is to know what has been unknown. However, to see a substantial state as it actually is requires universal, global, and social views that comply with the truth gained with views to see the truth and to see at large, and yet, humans lack such abilities, unified view, or methodology. Scientists, therefore, study science based on their own view or beliefs, but not on wisdom to understand today's complicated society in a comprehensive way. Especially a problem is social science that specializes in studying the society in question.

Different from natural science, the objects of social science study do not repeat themselves nor show accurate laws, hardly limiting the study. If each scientist continues their own study without a unifying view or methodology, the possibility of unifying understanding by the progress of science will never happen. But more scientists with different opinions will appear, only accelerating society getting more complicated.

Creating information without contents like scallion skins without the fruit is merely pollution. Of course, profit-minded mass media, or capitalism itself, is also responsible for this. However, also responsible are philosophy, science, ideology, religions, and everything else that has accepted the distorted giant reality without recognizing the relationship between the conception and the actual state that has been preposterous since the start of civilization, and have sought the truth believing the reality is only where they can find it. Therefore, most of the knowledge about social relationships today have formed an opposite relationship with the truth, and there is a gap between the reality. This gap was caused because they believe society is difficult to grasp or understand, denying that they are wrong, and they try to continue on the same path. Here lies the vicious cycle of thinking. And here also lies the reason they do not realize the simple fact that the existence of humans is the beginning of everything.

If humans do not exist, society, science, ideology, and civilization that involve humans do not exist as well. This simple and natural fact should be reconsidered to establish the knowledge as the truth that complies with the reality. Even if we are not good at this process, we need to inquire again about humans, society, and nature, clarify our existence and its meaning, as well as the position in the relationship with the great nature, and know the characteristics, directions, limits of the vessel that contains humans. Only then should we reconsider the problems that have occurred within the society: otherwise, we cannot free ourselves from the vicious cycle of seeking. The fact that this process is difficult, and that we are not good at it has been proven by many people who have tried to do so without any success. However, it is not a problem we should leave alone. If we do, this vicious cycle of thinking will develop into a grave problem of extinction of all human beings. Therefore, we should shift our attitude of leaving this problem to some scholars, but to the attitude that we all address it as the problem for all human beings.

6. Absence of Philosophy

I have explained various examples of human ideologies and attitudes that have derived from ignorance. Considering these deeply, I find that all these have occurred due to the absence of philosophy. As I will the explain details in the next chapter, humans have transformed themselves into the existence that can live only with their brains with the occurrence of civilization. The cause of all the problems is that the human brain, the very support, has become ineffective in leading the increasingly complicated society.

The brain means science and philosophy. Originally, science should be established upon a firm and unified philosophy and at the same time conducted under the control of philosophy, otherwise science is diversified, and becomes unable to unify matters and becomes incomprehensive as a whole.

Then, why doesn't firm and unified philosophy appear? Why is such philosophy absent? To think deeply about cause, the absence of a view that covers the whole history and that encompasses the whole, and seeing the population only on one side, and the human brain being dual structured are the fundamental reasons.

I would like to describe the details.

A. Absence of Views That Covers the Whole History

It is said that human history is about 2 million years, of which about 1.99 million years except the 10,000 years since civilization, or as long as 99.5%, provided primitive life to humans. Today, most people see the long human life before civilization as wild and abnormal, while the short 10,000 years after civilization, or 0.5% of the whole history, as humane, civilized, and normal life. Why do they seek the meaning of everything only within the small, civilized society and short civilized time like the frog in the well? The reason why we don't understand anything is due to these narrow views and thinking. Even when social scientists who are specialized in sociology review the history to learn how humans should be and live, most of them have seen only the history after civilization.

Essentially, social scientists should have given a consistent view to the human history, or even the whole history of living organisms of over 3 billion years, but they have ignored the area probably thinking that it is the area for archeologists and biologists. They seek answers only within the range of civilization considering that learning about primitive humans is meaningless as if humans after civilization are a totally a new species. There is no view of covering the whole history. Considering the short history after civilization against the 2 million years of human history, the history after civilization is unique and abnormal. It is reasonable to understand the true life of humans as animals is the life of 1.99 million years before civilization and the short history after civilization is only its variation. However, they see history from the side of history after civilization which is only one point in history. Their view and idea of the world have become misplaced, feet not on the ground, and inconsistent, making a vicious cycle. Today's humans are the result of a long history. Without complying with the fact, we can never understand the logic of nature and live a proper life. It is as if looking at a tree at its branches and leaves without seeing its trunk or roots. Such a way of thinking will stay in a vicious cycle never reaching the trunk or roots.

The lifestyle based on such ideology naturally makes the whole society create a gap with the natural logic, leading the second lifestyle to a deadlock, that is where we stand today. To see the true history, we need to have a consistent view of the whole history from its headstream, and try to understand the essence hidden in the shade of phenomenon.

B. Absence of Views that Encompass the Whole

How should a correct human life be after starting to use their brain? That is to know nature from its side both broadly and essentially, and also know the circumstances of humans, then adapt themselves to nature in a selfless, strict, and neutral manner. In other words, human ancestors and other animals lived a life that could continue eternally by adapting themselves to nature without reasoning, but on the other hand, humans who started to depend on their brain are required to know the nature both broadly and essentially in selfless, strict, and neutral manner, as well as to know themselves and then adapting themselves to nature with complete reasoning of the human side.

Living organisms born from nature cannot live without adapting themselves to their mother nature. Nature is selfless, strict, and neutral. Nature has a rule that it only nurtures living organisms that adapt themselves either by instinct or by brain, and eliminates any life that does not adapt.

There are two ways to adapt ourselves to mother nature and continue to survive as an eternal species.

One is to live by adapting ourselves by our instincts without reasoning.

All organisms except humans have adapted themselves to nature this way for hundreds of millions or billions of years. Humans had lived in the same way until 10,000 years ago.

The second way is to know everything about the logic of nature by brain and also about ourselves, and then adapting ourselves to nature with our initiative. Humans became an animal that can live depending only on the brain 10,000 years ago. However, humans have not reached the stage of this second way where they have understood the logic of both nature and humans by brain and adapt themselves to nature with their initiative to remain forever. Currently humans live neither in the first nor the second way, but somewhere in the middle. A species that does not devote itself to either one of the two ways, will not be selected by nature and go extinct. Here lies the essence of the danger caused by the inability of humans to adapt themselves to the logic of nature. However, humans have come too far to this stage to go back to the beginning.

The only way for survival and eternal existence left for humans is the second way with thorough use of the brain. Therefore, humans have to make the latent philosophical cognition ability appear immediately and try to actually adapt themselves to nature. Today's humans are overconfident believing that they can create various things by using scientific technology and that nothing is impossible. However, scientific technology is merely the application of natural law and just an imitation. Humans can enhance scientific technology to higher levels, but they can never create natural law. They should remember they cannot go beyond nature.

Also, humans have physiologic functions, and should understand that they can live only under certain restrictions of the natural environment. From this point as well, humans have no other choice than the second way to live.

The meaning of the true way of life through evolution of the brain also means a life of adapting to nature while making good use of the brain, not through developing only the scientific cognition ability and living recklessly.

This is a particularly important part. This may repeat what I am saying, but I would like to share the sentences I wrote from the same angle.

We humans were born on this earth and live on it as our mother. The earth, our land, hardly changes and we assume it will live 4.5 billion more years. Therefore, as long as we are careful, humans can stay on earth for almost eternally on earth.

As I have stated above, strictly neutral never-changing logic (never forced to move by intentions or emotions of someone) functions in nature. To keep a species' existence in such nature eternally (until the time the natural environment changes too drastically for the species to adapt to), there are only two ways of living.

The first way of living is to live keeping good balance totally instinctively under the logic and law of nature.

The second way of living is not the way like today to live adapting ourselves to the logic and law of nature (humans society is controlled over these) blindly with fragment knowledge and ideas not knowing about the future and fate in the future, but to live foreseeing the outcome of our current living, understanding natural logic essentially, and having the ability beyond nature (intelligent way of life). In other words, nature is the mother of living beings, but it has strictly neutral logic and laws, maintaining a strict stance. It has the power to end species that do not adapt perfectly to natural logic and laws. For a species to exist forever in such nature, there are only two ways of living; to keep balance instinctively to nature with complete ignorance, or to control the balance reasonably with complete intelligence and ability beyond nature.

The ones who live the first lifestyle are wild animals. They follow natural law, not planting nor harvesting, and their life will never end. Actually, humans had such a lifestyle for as long as 2 million years since the beginning until just recently. If humans had not been highly intelligent and had not broken the natural law as they did 10,000 years ago, maintaining the primitive life as they had for 2 million years, humans would have had eternal life. However, as they had some reasons I will explain later, 10,000 years ago and with a little intelligence they developed, they shifted their lifestyle to depend on their wisdom out of necessity. Then, until today, they have been able to remain present with their wisdom. During that time, they did not grow out of the first lifestyle, nor did they reach the second lifestyle. With the intermediate lifestyle between the first and second lifestyle, it is impossible to obtain eternal existence from the point of natural logic. Today's humans live this intermediate lifestyle.

Because the brain today has not fully developed and become unreliable, civilized society has reached the deadlock and is facing danger. Even if we cannot be optimistic, we have hope. Humans have evolved themselves to survive using the brain as a result of not the hope of humans but the direction of evolution. As I explained earlier, nature is selfless, strict, and neutral. It is impossible that evolution is affecting negatively only humans. Therefore, eternal existence with lifestyle depending on the brain cannot be impossible.

Now the brain of individual humans has developed wonderfully to understand various meanings, except that they are not used in a true sense due to the lack of unified cognition that covers the logic of nature, society, and humans, or in other words philosophy. Therefore, if the philosophy that covers the logic of nature, society, and humans is developed, and based on this developed logic, if the human society operation program is created, and then if the future civilized society will become a society led by intelligence, humans can exist with the brain forever. This philosophy is what I have been explaining here. Therefore, humans are already on the stage of obtaining their lifestyle.

C. Population is seen only one-sidedly

To us humans today, problems within society are much bigger than problems in nature. This is why social study is needed more than ever. When we say simply what society is, we can say society is a group of human beings. Then society is not formed without a group of human beings, or population, and population is the most basic element of forming a society. In this course of thought, every problem in society is deeply related to population. There is no problem that is not affected by the increase or decrease of population. Therefore, to consider various problems of modern society, ignoring or looking lightly on the increase of population produces unsatisfactory answers. Then do scholars study society placing much importance on this most grave population problem? Unfortunately, the answer is not really. The reason that primitive society collapsed and developed into civilized society and the cause of the civilized society expanding and developing to date, as well as the cause the civilized society is at the point of being questioned if it can shift to the next form of society are, to see them closely, all from the common condition, that is increased population. In other words, the fundamental condition of expanding and developing society from primitive to future times is population and its increase. Therefore, to accurately understand society systematically, the problem of population increase that is the fundamental condition for expansion should never be seen lightly or ignored. However, not just ordinary people but philosophers and social scientists have seen this most important problem of population increase lightly or ignored it. They only looked at society with minor conditions and concluded that they do not understand society. It is the same as you stepping on one foot with the other foot and saying you cannot move the foot; a natural consequence.

The confusion of today's society and uncertainty of future society are caused by the actual absence of philosophers and social scientists. All professional philosophers and social scientists around the world should reflect on their negligence and make a fresh start. I emphasized population, but of course there are other important elements such as food, to be provided to the population. However, if we study the population issue deeper, other elements will also be understood in connection with the population, and eventually the essence of civilized society will also be understood. Therefore, it is the worst mistake that population, the most fundamental element, has been overlooked, or observed only on one side.

Philosophers and social scientist have seen the increasing population in a coherent manner as progress, and not just seeing it on the surface so far. They have not tried to discover the meaning hidden there, but just deal with various phenomena such as birthrates, deathrates, or the population of labors and elderly people, to obtain statistics.

Then, why didn't humans see the grave teaching or other sides that gives us hints? I can only say that this is because the human brain is dual-structured. Cognitive ability of humans is good at understanding actual science but less capable of understanding essential science.

Population has kept growing using the principle of expanding circulation of population, food, and the brain for 2 million years on this earth as water fills a bucket. At the same time, society has kept expanding and becoming complicated. In other words, human history has always been a history of population issue, as well as a history of solving the problem. Philosophers and social scientists did not try to see the process, but, as I have already written, they have been studying the birthrates, labor populations, or other similar subjects. They see the river of population at its cross section only when they could have seen it as one flow.

This is because most scholars have demonstrated their scientific cognitive ability only. A study of the cross section of the river of population with this scientific cognitive ability, will not help them to understand the entire river of population flowing in the phenomena of society. It can be understood only by the philosophical cognitive ability that corresponds to the river of population. Population is the beginning of everything, and also the end of everything. Also, population is the foundation of society, and the motivating power of everything, bearing the role of the pivot of a fan. The fact that they have seen population only from one perspective is the biggest reason, among all the reasons, of the absence of philosophy.

D. Human brain is dual structured

All causes that destroy humans of today lie in humans themselves, not the earth or other animals. And further, that is in the ignorance of human brain. Humans do not realize this fact yet in a true sense. It is a paradox that humans are facing the dangerous point of destruction but not realize that because they are ignorant. There is nothing more dangerous than ignorance, and this is caused by the dual structure of the human brain.

That human brain is dual structured, meaning cognition ability is dual structured. One of the dual structured cognition abilities is the ability to recognize things in actual, concrete, and scientific concepts with five senses. The other is the ability to recognize things in essential, abstract, and philosophical concepts.

Hereinafter, I will call the former the scientific cognition ability, and the latter the philosophical cognition ability.

Until today, the former cognition ability is far better than the latter ability in humans. In other words, humans have been strong at using the scientific cognition ability, and weak at using the philosophical cognition ability. Therefore, with this strong scientific cognition ability, humans have used and applied nature for themselves. However, due to the weakness in the philosophical cognition ability, they have not found the true meaning why humans were civilized, or the direction humans should lead civilized society to. Here lies the reason why humans who have survived with the brain cannot be intermeshed with nature, in other words, they have no other way than to become extinct.

This undisplayed philosophical cognition ability should have appeared to control the scientific cognition ability and let both abilities the true brain of humans. Due to the lack of philosophical cognition ability, this most important aspect has not been recognized, as well as other various matters I have discussed and will discuss later.

I have explained the four causes of the lack of philosophy. Absence of a view that covers the whole history, absence of view that encompasses the whole, and the one-sided view of population are, after all, caused by lack of this philosophical cognition ability, and the fundamental cause of absence of philosophy is the dual structured brain of humans.

Chapter 3. Shift to Humans Living with Brain

1. Civilization and Brain

Now I would like to get down to the main discussion.

In ancient times, humans lived adapting themselves instinctively to nature, but transformed themselves to live using their brain about 10,000 years ago. For about 2 million years until 10,000 years ago, humans lived in groups eating natural food collected in nature. After that they started using the brain to apply natural law to agriculture and farming to secure food, formed organized society, and shifted their lifestyle to adapting themselves to society. It was the point when humans started to survive only by using the brain. In other words, the fate of humans changed after that. It depends on their own brain if they can survive or go extinct.

Humans did not know clearly that they changed their fate, but in any case, they have lived using their brain for about 10,000 years so far. This is particularly important, so I would like to go a little more in detail. Humans appeared in one area of Africa about 2 million years ago. At that time, they finally shifted their life on trees to the life on the ground, and since then with evolution of their legs, their brain evolved straight ahead. This evolution is called orthogenesis, with which the brain would replace instinct to take the leading role of life if evolution continues. And that happened in reality 1.99 billion years after the appearance of humans, or 10,000 years ago. To say specifically, that happened by the logic of expanding circulation of population, food, and brain. Population in 2 million years ago is considered to be about 500. Under the strict natural selection force, population increased by 0.5 person a year, to become about one million by 1.99 billion years ago.

They depended on nature for food. It is thought that other animals bigger than humans did not increase like humans who used evolved brains to adapt themselves to the environment and dispersed themselves to all corners on the earth. The population had the tendency to increase further, but with the limitation of natural food, nature limited humans to be the population of about one million. It was the most struggling time in history for humans, but it was because of this struggling that promoted civilization. In other words, they had brains that were developed at almost the same level as we have, with which they applied natural law to produce food and a new lifestyle to be civilized out of necessity. However, modern people are not aware of the fact that this process changed the fate of humans.

Once humans shifted to a new civilized lifestyle, due to the rapid population increase and evolution of social systemization, they became fated to be irreversible not being able to return to the old natural lifestyle. In other words, before knowing it, humans found themselves to have the fate to live depending on their brain since they shifted to a new lifestyle. They changed their fate to depend on their brain whether they can survive or not.

Humans have never recognized clearly that they changed their fate, but in any case they have survived by using their brain. However, the brain is incomplete and far from forever dependable. Therefore, humans became unable to adapt themselves to highly developed, highly completed civilized society, making their ideology go into a vicious circulation and getting forced to be buried in society. This is as if humans who cannot live only with the brain are tested how long they can survive. They have reached the situation where they have their swords broken, no more arrows, and no other choice than surrender to nature. Since humans changed their lifestyle 10,000 years ago to have no other way than to go extinct when they cannot live with their brain any longer, they are facing the biggest crisis (the second crisis since the end of the primitive times).

However, we should give it more careful consideration. Nature is selfless, strict, and neutral. Humans changed their lifestyle to live with the brain not by their own will but by natural law. In other words, humans changed their lifestyle to live with the brain as a result of evolution. We can say that nature created humans to be capable of living with the brain because the foundation where humans can exist forever complying with natural principles and also with their brain was ready. Therefore, we do not need to be pessimistic, but can be optimistic. Humans can exist forever with the brain. The problem is how we can understand nature and ourselves with this brain.

The difficulty of this problem caused today's situation, but the logic of eternity exists in nature. Therefore, if we try to understand with the philosophical cognition ability, we can obtain the logic. If we obtain the logic with this ability and control society, we can obtain the true brain that evolves, and make it exist forever. However, in reality, only the scientific cognition ability is working. Before going in detail about the relationship between philosophy and science, I would like to discuss the reality of this flight on only one engine, in other words, the reality of reckless driving of scientific civilization in absence of philosophy.

2. Scientific Civilization in Absence of Philosophy

With great development of scientific technology, civilization made a drastic development, but development of scientific technology is only academic development, or development of the brain. Various studies have developed sub-sections making more sub-sections, solving problems of a wide range. This means humans have obtained wisdom and are equipped with the ability to survive, but still, humans cannot avoid extinction if this condition continues. Why is that? Besides, why can't any scholar provide effective solutions?

As I consider, this possibility of extinction is growing along with the improvement of studies. This is only because studies have been established wrongly completely. No one has said what is wrong, but I am sure that is caused by wrong studies. Further studies which are about the brains of humans who can live only with brain's development, the closer humans proceed toward extinction. What else has such a huge contradiction? This is because of absence of philosophy, and also because of the imperfect brain that is the mother of civilization. If I can add, it is because of the flight with a single engine by a dual structured brain.

Today we are developing new knowledge with science and we live depending on science. We also believe we have to rely on science in the future. However, today's problems have been caused because science is unreliable. If we still have to depend on science, the question is what the problem with science is. To this question, the flight with a single engine theory gives us the answer.

I would like to discuss slowly without extreme expressions.

The life of a person is generally decided depending on the society and the era he is born into. Either born to an undeveloped primitive society, or to a highly civilized society, it is the place of his life and the world to him. Then, what kind of society do we currently live in? I would like to discuss this for clear understanding.

We can say that the society we live in now is a society of scientific civilization made with highly developed scientific technology. According to a newspaper article, if the scientific technology established by humans for thousands of years to 1945 is made in a graph, the height would be 9cm. However, the height for 15 years after that to 1960 would be equal to the height of a 13-story building. It may sound like an exaggeration, but the development of modern scientific technology is so resounding. We know the successful result of modern scientific technology in jumbo jets, computers, satellites, and nuclear weapons. Closer to us are motorization and home electric appliances. However, these are only a several hundredth of actual scientific technology. Developments in the area not in our daily life or we do not see or hear are much larger. Thanks to those scientific technological developments, our lives have surely become greatly more efficient, wealthier, and happier. We also gave our absolute trust in scientific technology and even more expectations for it.

However, the happiness and expectations did not last long. Modern civilization developed by scientific technology started to show great distortion and maladies, and we realized that scientific technology is not entirely absolute nor a friend of humans. Scientific technology is originally neutral and like a double-edged sword. It can give humans either positive or negative consequences depending on the humans who use it. Scientific technology is faceless. When it was used by humans who do not know the correct use of it, it started to show its maladies clearly. They include Japan's traffic disasters that create one casualty in one hundred people every year, air pollution from exhaust gas, factory soot, home dust, and water pollution from industrial and home wastewater. These are only a facial aspect of terror. Even more terror is that due to our ignorance we overthrust scientific technology one-sidedly, harming our finite mother earth with about 3.9 billion people, destroying it with tremendous energy.

If humans continue to use scientific technology haphazardly based on the desires of each person without checking the earth's accommodation ability and cyclical function, it is clear that the earth will be destroyed, and we will be unable to live there anymore. We should recognize this as the most fearful force of natural selection that will occur more certainly than any war. Also, if we see the effects of scientific technology from another angle, we see that it is giving a drastic change to civilization generally. In the civilized society developed by the motive power of scientific technology, everything is reaching the limit of diversity, acceleration, and complication. People cannot follow such a society; their ideology has come to the deadlock and fallen in a stuporous state. For example, in this drastically transforming society, teachers and all leaders of the world cannot share a common view, making discussions going in a vicious cycle. Of course, the same can be said for the operation of economy and politics. Some of the young generation have gone escapistic or pessimistic and become hippies, while others have become violent or rebellious and have become campus activists.

Due to the drastic changes, most people have lost the basic understanding of the society they live in and where society is heading to.

As explained above, humans are facing the crisis due to their own ignorance and to scientific technology they created. The gravity of the crisis is gaining its speed. Social technology is supposed to have been developed for humans, then why do humans have to suffer? Then, if scientific technology is a neutral and double-edged sword to humans, why don't we solve this problem with philosophy or science and use it without bringing negative effects? Anyone can question this point and wonder.

Today, many intellectuals around the world are trying to solve this problem, but their thinking has come to a deadlock and is going in a vicious cycle. Why has this society become so difficult? Some people think as follows.

Society used to be slow and strongly controlled by a spiritual component, so people had to be mentally prepared to comply with the modern scientific civilization they experience for the first time and had to establish the way to control the society, but modern scientific civilization arrived rapidly like angry water before establishing the way and the preparation was not completed in time. Therefore, the spiritual aspect of humans is in confusion today, and people cannot make an accurate judgement.

When society was simple, simple controls could work satisfactorily. Such societies also have a relatively stable auto-adjustment function working effectively. Simple and explorative thinking could somehow work satisfactorily by trials and errors. However, a dynamic society that changes drastically like today has, even with a relatively stable auto-adjustment function working, becomes a self-operating entity and we cannot depend on it anymore.

Here lies the bewildering confusion.

However, humans have reached today's highly developed society from primitive society via elementary-level society by the power of the brain that denied depending on instincts like other animals. Under today's circumstances of crisis, after all, we are fated to live by solving and overcoming problems with this power of brain. For this purpose, we need deep and wide, systematic ideology that can correspond to modern, rapidly changing scientific civilization. Such ideology has to be established by social science that corresponds to natural science that promotes modern civilization.

Today, very few people advocate what I have discussed. However, not many people discuss what I am going to discuss next. There are people who have realized that the key to solving problems is a drastic development of social science, but few people can concretely discuss how the development is possible.

3. Philosophy and Science

Today, the experiments to unify the excessively subdivided science fields into one powerful science that can correspond to the needs of modern society are active. Indeed, there should be far more merits than demerits for such experiments, and that neighboring divisions of science that are connected with each other, and should be unified together if possible, and work together rather than each individual division of science being independent.

However, the unification of science under the absence of philosophy or unified recognition would be exceedingly more difficult than said. That would be difficult technically, but the contents have even more difficult aspects. Even if the unification is conducted formally, we will not know if it is a genuine unification unless we compare it with the truth, herein lies the dilemma, we cannot compare it with the truth that is not available. Therefore, the unification of science today in the absence of philosophy has from the start only the possibility of ending up only gathering individual science divisions. This can especially be said for social science. We can see how difficult it is when we see small examples. For example, to see if it is possible for someone who has never seen roof tiles, pillars, tatami-mats, wall materials, doors, paper sliding screens, glasses, wooden boards, sliding doors, foundations, or any cluttered parts like individual science, can compile a concept of a house, it would be impossible. On the other hand, a person who has built or has seen a house being built could compile a concept of a house easily when he sees them. Therefore, without philosophy or blueprint, it is almost impossible to achieve true unification or compile a concept.

Furthermore, we should not overlook the weakness that a simple unification does not bear the concept of values. Indeed, the weak point of modern science is that it does not have philosophy.

Then, is it possible to find the unified cognition, in other words philosophy, under which to unify it as true science and systemize it? The answer would be that is surely possible. Such philosophy exists and is available to anyone. I would like to discuss the philosophy briefly, and then philosophy and science.

All phenomena occurring in human society are seen as natural occurrences, but they occur because humans exist, and do not occur if humans do not exist. Therefore, today's society has become complicated with all problems being interconnected like a tangled thread not showing the proper order, but if we follow the occurrence process systematically from the origin of humans' existence and give it a good thinking, they are clearly recognizable. If we compare today's human society to a tree, it is not a young tree but a grown tree with densely grown branches and leaves. The trunk of the tree, or society, represents humans, and this tree budded when humans appeared on earth. Then it grew with the increase of population, bore branches and leaves as human activities grew complicated, to grow into today's grown up tree. Humans have not kept their own history in a tree-like form, but if they were to do so, it would be similar to a tree that has kept the record of its history until it withers and dies out. Indeed, a completed tree represents the historical process and present state of humans.

We can easily understand the growth process of a tree systematically from a seed to grow to have branches and become a grown up tree. If we try to understand the historical process of humans from their origin as the growth process of a tree, we can understand everything clearly.

To think why a civilized society develops, we can start by considering scientific technology, economy, brain, desires, or any other elements. However, everyone comes to a deadlock in thinking. If we consider the logic of expanding the circulation of population, food, and brain, we never would reach such a deadlock. This is because it is the thinking from the fundamental, or original point. Everything starts because humans exist, and then everything becomes a problem. That thinking starts from this point. Even if we say the unified cognition can be obtained by anyone, there is an entrance of thinking like a pin hall when Apollo the spaceship entered into the atmosphere. That is, on the condition that if it does not miss its target.

Now I would like to discuss the problem of philosophy and science. So far we haven't had the idea of seeing the wide range of problems including population, food, economy, resources, environment, information, education, ideology, and wars, in one unified system. However, it is possible. At first glance, all of these phenomena seem to be occurring individually respectively, but from the beginning they occur like embryology. If we understand everything systematically like embryology, everything can be unified logically in systematic recognition. This is the natural way and correct way to see things.

Because all issues in social science that have studied humans and society were not established on the foundation of such unified recognition, not only studies were conducted respectively but also they could not be a complete science. In other words, the objects of scientific studies cannot be divided, and science had to be unified in the first place. However, there has been no unified principle, or philosophy, that recognizes undivided study subjects to be one unified science, as scientists have individually conducted their studies based on their own ideology. Therefore, science has been diversified, and never to form one completed science. Herein lies the reason why social science is far from useful but just acting as critics' comments when the civilization has reached its peak in its complexity and needs the help of social science most to go forward.

Social science is the brain of humans. For social science to work in its real sense as the human brain, it should be completed as soon as possible. For that purpose, we should understand philosophy as unified cognition, and systemize social science under this philosophy to make it a dependable unified science. Also, we can understand the relationship between philosophy and science as follows. Economics is said to be exceedingly difficult. That is because subjects of economics have no universal principles unlike physics or chemistry. Not only that, but the subjects of economic study are also the economical aspects of the society. If we do not understand society basically, economics cannot be independent as an academic subject. Professor Leontief, an American prestigious economist, said in a TV show, "Economics is still on the stage of philosophical searching," which I totally agree with.

The same can be said for other individual social science, because it is impossible that individual science divisions that study independent respective subjects in society can be firmly established while the general picture of society is not clear. For each individual science to become genuine science, society should first be recognized as a unified entity, and based on the unified recognition, science should be studied unitedly. So far, the whole picture of society has not been clear philosophically, and sociologists have conducted science not based on philosophy. Therefore, all social scientists have studied only by trial and error. In other words, unless the whole picture of society becomes clear, individual science divisions that specialize in respective parts can always study only by trial and error, and they can never become genuine science.

Science can be classified in two divisions: natural science that studies nature and social science that studies society. Of the two, the science that especially requires philosophy is social science due to the nature of the objects this science studies and values. The objects in natural science studies are static, change according to natural law, and repeat similar actions. Therefore, in natural science, each scientist can study their own field, and when the results are brought to be connected together, they can compile the unified principle that broadly corresponds to nature. On the contrary, the objects of social science studies are dynamic and it is a field where humans affect. It has no strict law, nor repetition. The objects hardly restrict the study. Therefore, under the absence of philosophy, if each scientist studies their own field like natural scientists do, and when the results are connected together, they end up compiling the science as it is today. In this way, social science should be supported by firm philosophy. Also, as I wrote that philosophy and social science are deeply related to each other by the issue of value, social science is primarily not the science that should stand equal to natural science. That is because natural science is, to be extreme, a science that only explores nature, while social science is a science of value of lifestyle of humans that covers wide variety of subjects from how humans should live, how humans should operate society, and how nature and humans should take balance, to how natural science should develop and be used, and present conclusions.

To go into more detail, it is the science that should create systems and policies for all humans to survive on this earth, and should be the head of all ideologies and actions. In other words, social science is the brain that works concretely for humans. Therefore, social science is not a science to take the same level from the standpoint as natural science, but should bear the leadership role. In reality, social science is far from successful, letting natural science enjoy its success, but needless to say, this is due to the absence of philosophy. Therefore, philosophy has a deep relationship with social science in two meanings: study objects and values. Because philosophy and social science are deeply related, I have purposefully described social science to be understood as science.

4. Social Science Can Flourish

The imbalance of two kinds of science occurs due to the absence of philosophy as I have already explained, but it is also the fact that the imbalance occurs from the difference of the study objects. I would like to explain the objects that allow the imbalance of the two kinds of science to develop. In that, the objects of social science that have been considered as disadvantages or weak points are actually the owner of extraordinarily strong points. Before going into details, I would like to present an interesting recognition. Today, there are many ways of views toward society that differ from person to person, but the views toward nature are almost unified without large variations. However, that was opposite in ancient times. Long time ago, the views toward nature differed from person to person, and the views toward society were more unified. This complete turnaround occurred by the complexity of society and great development of natural science. Society in old times was in small groups and simply structured, therefore people could understand each other without thinking in a complex way, but society has grown to be as difficult as it is civilized and complicated. If social science that focuses on studying society had greatly developed, society could have been seen unitedly, but the important social science has not been developed, society has remained to be seen differently from person to person.

On the contrary, to see the change of views toward nature, different from society, nature in old times and nature today have made almost no change. What has changed is the view toward it. In old times, natural science was not developed, and nature was seen only religiously or philosophically. Therefore, superstitions were remarkably rampant. Nature was seen differently from person to person, but as civilization occurred and natural science developed, nature started to be seen unitedly. As above, the views toward society and nature were reversed. It is interesting the reverse occurred with different reasons for the two. Society started to be seen differently from person to person because social science did not develop while society became complicated. Nature started to be seen unitedly because natural science made a remarkable development. In the end, they switched their stances. This shows it is possible that, like the complex nature was simplified by the development of natural science, complicated society can be simplified by the development of social science and seen unitedly. Actually, this is the theme I want to clarify in this book.

Science can be generally classified into two: natural science and social science, corresponding to their range of study objects being natural phenomenon and social phenomenon. Natural science is further divided into individual science including astronomy, physics, biology, medicine, engineering, agriculture, among others. Social science is also further divided into individual sciences that studies social phenomena such as economics, history, social studies, education, psychology, anthropology, literature, legal studies, politics, among others. Conversely, natural science and social science are the general names for these many individual fields of science. (I have already stated most of these matters in previous paragraphs, but I have described again as the nuances are somewhat different and also important.)

Why has social science not developed while natural science has made a drastic development, making the imbalance between the two kinds of science? Firstly, the world of nature, universe, and materials natural since studies are about the world where complex thinking or emotions are not involved, and it is the world that changes according to the law. Then it decides matters by quality, measures in quantity, and out of them as materials, they formulate hypotheses, try them in experiments minutely, and by proving the theory they reach to the law or logic. Also, most of the study objects of natural science have eternity, never hide away, so the scientists can calmly study. Anyone can obtain the same results from study or experiments. The objects look mysterious attracting scientists' interest, and there are infinite study materials.

On the contrary, the social phenomena, the study objects of social science, such as people's thinking, emotions, and actions, are mixed in disorder affecting each other, each area such as politics, economy, education, culture, among others, are connected in succession, besides, they are dynamic and not eternal, always making drastic changes. Therefore, they lack mysterious nature, not attracting scientists' interest so much. Therefore, social scientists do not devote themselves in having scientific attitudes, and the results are not successful either. Here lies the reason social science does not flourish while natural science has made a remarkable development. In other words, herein lies the imbalance of the two kinds of science. As a result, the results of natural science are very minute and clear, while the results of social science are mostly ambiguous and different from one scientist to others, making the future prediction impossible. Influenced by these two kinds of science, our common sense is imbalanced. The common sense concerning nature is getting more accurate than philosophers in old times, while the common-sense concerning society is very vague. Therefore, people cannot have a stable view toward the issue of how to live, as well as politics, economy, diplomacy, education, and all the other issues concerning society, being unable to develop their ideology out of the searching attitude that differs from one person to another. In this way, due to the imbalance of the development of two kinds of societies, our common sense has been formed distortedly. We have to let social science make up for the delay and have both kinds of science restore the balanced state. However, is it possible to make up for the delay while the delay was made because it has been impossible? As I already emphasized, I am sure that it is possible that social science, which studies the objects difficult to grasp develops rapidly.

I believe that there have been problems in the way how philosophers and scholars have conducted their thinking so far. Because all of them have fallen into this common snare by chance, they have been unable to have social science evolved so far. The objects of social science that are affected by wills, different from the objects in natural science, could not be understood with simple natural scientific methods in the first place. The objects of social science are deeply related with human existence itself, therefore they are related in the matter of time and space in succession. Nothing stands alone. However, social phenomena are all deeply related with the existence of humans. They have characteristics recognizable in succession and unitedly within themselves. Therefore, obtaining this recognition and making social science systemized based on it to be a unified science, and conduct studies systematically, immediately it will become possible to restore the balance with natural science. Furthermore, based on the unified recognition, if the two kinds of science are unified and develop as unified science, it will be the wisdom of humans, and it can promise the eternity of human existence. I would like to write a little more about the characteristics that can be obtained in succession, but I will detail further in Chapter 5.

Most of the study objects of natural science repeat actions in lawful manners, whereas all the objects of social science do not repeat actions in lawful manners. Therefore, compared to natural science, social science has been said to be the science which is difficult to conduct and has disadvantages. However, to see the society from the point of overall view and the occurrence order, we can see that the great law controls the society, and the society flows and changes around the law. Therefore, if we can understand the law correctly and develop our thinking accordingly, we can understand society altogether, or in succession one matter after another, and we can predict and make policies effectively. Society has more characteristics than natural science does.

Humans still do not know that, at the beginning of the civilized era, a grave law was born to cover the whole society, and we live while being controlled by the law. Therefore, people are not sure why civilized society operates by itself, gaining speed and complexity. With the law of society, if we understand the most basic matter within the society and develop the logic around it, we can see everything in society clearly. Of course, that completely corresponds to natural logic and law. We should have found it and developed it, but we couldn't. Here lies the cause of the social science development not completed and clarifying society has not been achieved.

Chapter 4. The Relationship Between the Earth and Humans

Before going into Chapter 4, I would like to summarize the previous chapter.

Humans transformed themselves from animals that can live only with their brain about 10,000 years ago. Since then, humans have been relying on their brain for their survival. However, the human brain is incomplete and dual-structured. While it is strong in scientific cognition ability, it lacks philosophical cognition ability. Today's ignorant attitudes and ideologies have occurred from the incompleteness of such a brain. Even if it is good with scientific cognition ability, it is weak in important social science. This is caused by the difference in study objects. Natural science is developing positively steered by the study objects, but social science goes the opposite way. Therefore, it is social science that needs philosophy due to these two facts.

However, the study objects of social science that have been considered exceedingly difficult have been discovered that they can be understood in succession as a unified entity. This is the summary of the previous chapter.

In Chapter 4, I would like to place the foundation to make the study objects of social science unified and clear.

1. The First Way of Life

The true mind and essence are extremely easy to understand at their early stages. When you are in elementary school, you can understand the minds of your classmates, but it gets more difficult to understand the mind of your friends as you go up to high school, university, and into adulthood. Understanding the essence of society also gets more difficult as the society increases its complexity. Therefore, when trying to elucidate the lifestyle of the complicated civilized society, learning from the primitive lifestyle that exposes the basics of lifestyle of humans has significant meaning. It is said that it was more than three billion years after a simple life forms appeared on earth, life evolved into more complicated organisms, and finally humans appeared. To say more precisely when and where humans appeared, the strongest theory is that it was about 2 million years ago on the African continent. And this theory explains why humans live around the world with respective different language and culture, as well as skin color and physical culture, as follows. Since the first appearance in Africa, humans have increased their population, and spread the sphere of life gradually to survive in search for natural food. As a result, humans covered the world. From there, in the process of adapting to the climate, geography, or other environmental conditions through generations, they changed into several races as we see today.

Most of the 2 million years of human the era was the era of the first way of life, or a primitive era. It is said that the population of humans 2 million years ago was about 500, though this is not certain. Then the population gradually grew. Humans in those days were still close to apes, with bodies covered with thick hair. Even so, by shifting the life of living on trees to living the ground, they started upright walking, and are considered that they gradually shifted their diet to be omnivorous eating plants, fruits, small animals, seaweed, and seafood. They lived in caves and in shades of rocks in small family groups with self-discipline, but they did not settle in one place but moved around in search of natural food. As such, humans in primitive times lived a natural life, and they were directly affected whenever the natural environment changed. Of course, even under such conditions, they must have known that the secret of living a better life in nature is not to go against the natural environment but to adapt themselves to it.

To think more carefully, humans were born from nature like any other animals, and see nature as their parents, but their parental nature is neutral. it does not provide them helping hands, nor do they care about the suffering of humans. The ones who could survived were those who could adapt themselves to natural environment as the saying goes, "God helps those who help themselves." In other words, humans could survive only by adapting themselves to the natural environment that gives them repeated deep freezes, typhoons, droughts, food shortages, epidemics, fierce animals, and other difficulties. Under such severe natural conditions, numerous primitive peoples must have been eliminated. To see the hardness of primitive life from the aspect of population, the estimated human population of about 100 people 2 million years ago became about 1 million after 1.99 million years, which is 10,000 years ago, when humans started the first step toward civilized society with the success of producing food through the development of agriculture and farming by applying natural law. During that time, the population increased by about 10,000 times, but this took about 1.99 million years, and the increase was 0.5 person a year on average.

Generally, even under the natural environment where several cases of natural selection occurs, animals tend to increase their number over the amount of food. Therefore, we can imagine how life in the primitive era was severe when we think of the unbelievable number of the average population increase of 0.5 person a year of 1.99 million years. It would have been good if, even under such conditions, humans developed their life step by step and gained today's civilization as accumulated experiences, but it wasn't. At the end of the primitive era after 1.99 million years, as many a muckle makes a muckle, as I have just discussed, the slight increase of population reached about 1 million, sparsely covering the earth, causing food shortage, and humans reached their first limit. This is similar to today's limit of civilization, and here lies the important teaching we need to learn truly.

There is another thing that developed very slowly like the increase of humans population as many a mickle makes a muckle. That is the human brain. The size of the human brain was at first about the size of today's gorillas'. Humans were considered to be hardly using tools but to be using only stones and wooden sticks. However, as human evolution took the direction in which they depend on their brain, during the several hundred thousand years fighting against natural selection force, the human brain has evolved toward a fixed direction. The lifestyle depending on instincts shifted to the lifestyle using the brain. To say in more details, they started to use fire, roasting meat, or warming themselves, and to manufacture tools to use natural stones and wooden sticks easier. They started to exchange words which was still like cipher. This development of brain is, as I will discuss later, the great help for humans to break their first deadlock.

2. The First Deadlock

Humans survived depending on natural food for 1.99 million years out of 2 million years of human history. Because a society of a large group was not suitable to feed on collected natural food that was found scattered sparsely on earth, societies of small groups were maintained to allow them free migration. To maintain such societies, when the population of a society was overgrown, they divided themselves into smaller groups just like bees to keep a society small. All animals tend to increase larger in number than the amount of food when other conditions are satisfied. Humans were no exception; gradually they increased in number to catch up with the amount of available food and then exceeded their availability. In this process, naturally, there were numerous numbers of society dividing. After long years since the first appearance in Africa, humans sparsely covered the whole surface of the earth in small societies. The population of that time was about 1 million. The population had a strong tendency to increase even further, but due to the limit of the earth that is the base of natural food, the population was restrained at about 1 million. That was the deadlock of the first way of living. It is unknown how long this deadlock remained, but life in those times is considered to be the hardest in the primitive era, because we can consider as follows.

The earth that is the base of natural food is a kind of container with limited capacity. Humans are contained in it. On the earth with limited capacity, if the humans contained in it tended to always increase indefinitely, that would have worked as pressure to the earth, and the pressure would have transformed itself to the indirect power of elimination. We can imagine a difficult condition for humans there. Under the condition where the population is controlled to be about 1 million due to the availability of natural food, many people must have died of hunger or from diseases. There must have been filicides and abortions conducted rampantly, or even eating humans. Conflicts must have occurred often among people and many of them must have died there.

When I think of the fact that more than 10,000 people are dying almost every day in today's developing areas such as Africa and southeast Asia, or the history of about two hundred and some decade years of

Japan's national isolation starting from the early Edo era to the end of it, I do not think this is never an exaggerated view. Japan, a small island country, shut out any communication with the rest of the world from the Edo era to the beginning of the Meiji era. It was a small, closed world, in other words, a model of the earth with a limited capacity. When we apply it to the real world of the earth, there is hardly any contradiction. In Japan, a small version of the world, population kept increasing since old times with the theory of the expanding circulation of humans, food, and brain. However, the availability of fields for cultivation eventually reached the limit, the availability of food reached the limit, and the population growth stopped at about 30 million.

For two hundred and decades of years since then, the population was held to the limit of available food, but during that time of our ancestors, many people died of hunger or from diseases one after another, and there were filicides and abortions, or they even ate human meat. Also, conflicts among people often occurred and people died endlessly. In this way, after all, such force of natural selection held the population to the available amount of food.

The first deadlock was reached by the overpopulation against the availability of natural food. Therefore, the severity was only natural. However, we can consider that this severe first deadlock situation invited the new second way of life out of necessity. Paradoxically, if this deadlock did not happen, civilization would not have happened, and humans would have been still living primitive lifestyle. I would like to discuss this theory in the next section.

3. Theory of Shifting to the Second Way of Life

There are three elements that made humans shift their lifestyle to the second way, or a civilized way of life. Of the three, I already mentioned population and food. However, it is clear that a shift does not happen only with those elements. There are many proofs of that around us. In the nature world, many animals remain as they have been when humans are suffering with overpopulation. Then, what reversed the relationship between nature and humans as long ago as 10,000 years ago? In other words, what was the cause of bringing the reverse relationship between nature and humans other than population and food? The answer is, as I mentioned earlier, brain. Humans can be considered to have developed toward a fixed direction as an animal that survives depending only on the brain. The human brain evolved along with the evolution of the physical body. It is said that the human body had already evolved to the figure almost the same as modern humans by the end of the primitive era.

Apart from the question whether the depending on the brain is good or bad, this brain, only developed in humans, is one of the three elements that showed great performance and reversed the relationship between nature and humans. If humans did not have this brain that can even use the natural law, even if the severe times continue due to overpopulation because of the earth's small capacity for humans, humans must have had to continue their primitive lifestyle like other animals eternally under the conditions of natural selection. If this had happened, unless the earth's capacity for humans changes, the population of humans on earth would be limited to about 1 million at most as it actually was about 10,000 years ago. However, fortunately, or unfortunately, only humans developed their brain to use nature and shifted to a civilized lifestyle. It should be easier for you to understand the following explanation with these three elements in mind.

Civilization has caused various problems today, but the essential question as to why humans were civilized is not asked, and therefore no answer is provided. With the simple thinking centered on civilized society that affirms the traditional way of thinking that evolution of the brain made it possible to live life with agriculture and farming, people only study civilization itself. Textbooks that are supposed to provide real education to children also provide information on how humans were civilized only from such point of view.

Of course, I do affirm the evolution of the brain, but the new way of life occurred because the deadlock under the condition where overpopulation and the brain evolution were met. To discuss in more specific way, at the end of the primitive era, the human brain had evolved highly, but through thousands, or tens of thousands of years, when struggling in the situation under overpopulation was repeated, brain development was even more accelerated, in my opinion. As a result, with the developed brain, humans obtained the control over natural law that had previously controlled them one-sidedly and made them follow. It also made humans possible to promote agriculture and farming, to produce food to be self-sufficient, and then to have a new lifestyle. I believe this is the theory humans shifted to civilization. In other words, the traditional common theory is that even the primitive life did not change so much, the human brain developed, and they shifted their lifestyle to a newer style gradually. However, I see that brain evolution does not always cause a shift to a newer lifestyle but the suffering situation urged the brain to evolve, and these two elements made humans shift to a newer lifestyle.

It is natural to say that civilization would not have occurred without brain evolution. Many other animal species are struggling to survive under the chronic overpopulation like humans in the primitive age. The reason why they cannot shift to a newer lifestyle is that basically their brain does not evolve like humans. Therefore, if the human brain had not evolved, they must have been living a primitive lifestyle under the control of natural law like any other animals. However, brain evolution does not immediately lead to shifting to a new lifestyle with agriculture and farming. We should see that the shift occurs only when the brain‘s evolution occurred in the situation where shifting is needed, or the necessity of shifting meets the progress of brain evolution.

People who live in uncivilized areas currently including Bushmen in Africa are said to have brain evolved almost to the same level as ours, and some of them even know agriculture and farming. The reason why they do not shift their lifestyle to a civilized way of cultivating plants or breeding livestock animals is said that they can find natural food enough for them. If the earth were hundreds times larger than the actual size, providing us far more food, having the ability of accommodating almost an infinite number of populations, it would be able to feed the increasing number of humans almost forever. Even if the human brain developed only slowly, no necessity for a cultivated lifestyle would have occurred, and humans would have been living primitive lives still in modern times. Therefore, the fact humans obtained the possibility of surviving with their brains in the process of evolution, and also the fact that the earth is rather small with limited capacity for population are the causes that led humans to shift to a new lifestyle. In other words, when the three elements - population growth, lack of food on the earth, and brain development – are all met, civilization occurred. And by seeing this way, we can solve the mystery of why humans were civilized after 1.99 million years out of 2 million years of their history as if the idea hit them suddenly.

The maximum food supply ability of the earth in natural conditions is supposed to be for 1 million people. By the fact that it took 1.99 million years until the population growth reached the maximum food supply, or until the population reached 1 million considering 0.5 person on average were added each year, we can start solving the mystery of why civilization occurred all of a sudden only at that point in history.

History is a great teacher. What gave me this view was also history. However, it was not the view of history that each event occurred after civilization phenomenally and descriptively, but the view of overall history to read the essence hidden under phenomenon.

4. Difference between the First and Second Ways of Life

At the end of the first way of life, increased population and food shortages caused an absolute overpopulation phenomenon, leading humans to a deadlock. Then the human brain was set free and humans shifted to the second way of life. I have explained that in the previous section. I would like to discuss what occurred after that.

The reason why humans came to a deadlock in the first way of life was food shortage against the population. The fact humans became free from the problem obviously means humans secured available food over population. However, as I stated previously, population tends to grow exceeding the amount of available food if other conditions allow. Solution of food shortage was not absolute but a relative solution between population and available food like a see-saw game. Seeing this way, we can say that the second way of life was based on logic not basically different from the first way of life. Some differences occurred between the two lifestyles that the first lifestyle was spreading the population sparsely around the world whereas the second lifestyle was to live densely on the same earth. I would like to list the differences between the first and second ways of life.

The first difference is the production of food by humans. Humans have depended on natural food for about 2 million years, most of their history, but due to the reasons I stated previously, they have depended on food they produce since 10,000 years ago. It is a well-known fact that this production of food by humans is the foundation of civilized society.

The second difference is settlement. Humans' food production was with both agriculture and farming, but agriculture was primary. Usually, it is conducted on a fixed land, requiring people to shift their mobile lifestyle to a settling lifestyle. Therefore, humans started settling with the start of agriculture.

The third difference is from division to aggregation. In the primitive era, as people moved around collecting natural food, society of a small group was more convenient, and they avoided letting the society grow bigger. However, since they started agriculture, such problem was solved, and it became even convenient for them to make larger groups to perform agriculture that require cooperation of people, and further, as people started to store food and properties gained from agriculture and breeding livestock animals, inviting constant conflicts with other groups, it became convenient to make the group bigger and stronger, each group started to make aggregated and larger. Large groups here mean large families in some cases, but mostly groups of collection of families.

The fourth difference is organization and politics. As groups grow larger, requiring agriculture conducted reasonably, they require organization and politics, gradually creating different organizations and systems corresponding to the new lifestyle in the group. Today's complicated organizations, systems, and politics are the extension of all these frontlines.

The fifth difference is diversity and advancement. Necessity in various matters for the new lifestyle, agriculture, and farming, development and improvement of new agricultural tools and daily commodities occurred, accompanied by diversity of intelligence and desires, becoming the foundation of today's civilization of materials and information.

The sixth difference is society becoming second nature. As agricultural life settled, as I wrote previously, society became the second nature to humans, and further, a fortress. Humans used to live adapting themselves directly to severe nature, but they shifted their lifestyle where they can survive if they can only adapt themselves to society, and adapting to nature through society. Society became their second nature, or fortress.

The seventh difference is the society that has its own law and it operates by itself. Before civilization, humans lived adapting themselves directly to nature. Society existed only for convenience, being just as a group of people. However, after civilization, society became their second nature, a fortress. Society became quite different in quality. Furthermore, as people started to live performing circulating economical activities only within society, this society started to have functions as the law and marketability. When the society is controlled and operated under a perfect order as planned, this law is controlled and has no room to perform its power, but when it is not, the law performs its power according to the level of development in planning. When society is complicated, and people in the society do not have much power to govern it, the law leads society to perform its self-operation ability on behalf of the people. Incompetent people consider this ability as convenient and welcome this steering power of society. They fall under the delusion that adapting themselves to the power is the desired way, misplacing their priorities.

Unless humans learn everything, regain perfect control, operate society in a coordinated way with human principles, and have control over the power, humans will be innocently led by the power to the grave. Today, the situation for most humans is as if they are sitting comfortably on an express train running toward their grave.

The eighth difference is living sparsely and densely. As I mentioned previously, before civilization, humans lived scattered sparsely around the world, but after civilization they started to cover densely on that same earth. However, this living densely does not guarantee stability, because another deadlock is inevitable. I will discuss this later, but to explain the reason, that is because while the earth has limits in every way, population grows with the theory of expanding circulation of population, food, and brain, filling out the earth's capacity soon is inevitable from the start. Even though humans succeeded in living densely, the second way of life has a limit itself. In other words, the new lifestyle was made possible by overcoming the problems of the first lifestyle, but this second lifestyle is fated to have problems again. This is only natural because, while the earth has a limited capacity, the theory of expanding circulation of population, food, and brain remains the same. The deadlock happening today occurred as a consequence.

The ninth difference is that humans shifted to the lifestyle with the brain. As I stated previously, at the end of the primitive era, absolute overpopulation and development of the brain caused civilization. However, humans shifted their lifestyle with which they can survive only by depending on their brain. In other words, they have changed their fate to be depending on their own brain. Humans have not recognized this clearly, but they have managed to survive with their brain. However, the brain reached its deadlock, and the human fate has become gloomy. However, humans should not give in to fate.

As described above, various differences are seen between the first and the second lifestyles, but I should add that the foundation has hardly changed.

5. The Commonality of the First and Second Ways of Life

I discussed the differences between the first and the second ways of life in the previous section, and in this section, I would like to discuss their commonalities.

The first commonality is that everyone lives with the desire to live, not to die, as long as he is born to this world. No one was born with his own will. However, once he is born, he lives supported inexplicably by the desire to live, not to die. Some people awake to themselves and want to commit suicide due to various reasons, but this fact does not deny this commonality. The commonality I discuss here is that it is not only common both to the first and second lifestyles but also the desire is universal. The desire of humans to live never changes as long as humans stay on this earth.

The second commonality is that humans have to eat to live. All living organisms cannot live without repeating the actions of taking food from the environment and emitting the waste to the environment. In reality, not just food but we should also include water and air; they are all universal.

The third commonality is the instinct of preservation of species. The basic condition for all living organisms flourish avoiding extinction is to have this instinct to preserve their own species. Humans are no exception. Birth control seen recently is not a counteract of prosperity of the species, but rather, it is a self-adjustment to allow the species to prosper eternally.

The fourth commonality is the evolution of the brain to a fixed direction. I have discussed this matter several times so far. When we talk about brain evolution today, there are two meanings I have to explain. One is the biological brain evolution, and the other is cultural brain evolution. The biological brain evolution is the evolution of the brain itself, and the cultural brain evolution is the evolution by information. The evolution I am talking about is the biological brain evolution. It evolves quite slowly, but it is evolving without stopping. It is said that if children in a primitive area are brought to a civilized society and get them used to the new lifestyle, they show almost the same intelligence as children brought up in a civilized society. Even under a natural environment, their biological brain shows the same level of development as ours.

The fifth commonality is that the size and the characteristics of the earth which will never change. I will discuss this matter later in "Characteristics of Nature".

The sixth commonality is that nature lets organisms that adapt themselves to nature survive, and let organisms that don't adapt go extinct. All living organisms are born from mother nature, and they can live only by adapting themselves to mother nature. This is the law of nature. I will explain this in the next section.

The seventh commonality is the humans' limit in the ability of adapting to the environment. Natural environment keeps changing to aggressive human activities. Humans, who are born from it and can survive only by adapting to it, cannot change themselves freely to catch up with the change of the natural environment. Humans are children of nature, but at the same time, they are independent and one united entity with one environment that is like an ecosystem. I call it the internal environment of humans. The adapting ability of this internal environment has a limit. I will discuss this matter in detail in the "Characteristics of Nature".

The eighth commonality is the universality of expanding circulation theory of population, food, and brain. This theory controls humans consistently both in the primitive and civilized eras and also in the future, or as long as humans exist. What made humans in primitive era prosper in population to the limit of the earth, and what made humans broke through this limit to civilization was this theory. Furthermore, what made the civilization prosper more than ever reaching the second limit is also this theory. Probably there is nothing that cannot be explained with this theory. Of course, with this theory, it is also possible to find the reason for today's deadlock, its solution, and to discover a new lifestyle. That is because this is the fundamental theory of everything in society.

As stated above, fundamental issues remain common how different times go. Therefore, as we try to understand focusing on this point, we can understand the social structure, our priorities, and the ideal way of life however complicated society develops.

6. The Second Way of Life

In this section, I would like to list only the distinctive features after civilization, or in the second way of life.

A. Humans Adapting Only to Society

In the primitive era, humans adapted themselves to nature itself, but people in the era after civilization live adapting themselves only to civilized society because society became the second natural environment that satisfied their needs. This society becoming second nature to them was established gradually in the process of civilization, and therefore people accepted the process quite naturally.

As a result, civilized people take it for granted to adapt themselves to society that is second nature, just like primitive people took it for granted to adapt themselves to nature, therefore they have forgotten their original relationship with nature.

In other words, after the establishment of civilization humans stopped adapting themselves directly to nature like primitive people and other animals, but they adapted themselves only to society, or their second nature. In this way, it has now become natural and a common sense that we adapt ourselves to society, but at the same time, the relationship between us and society is that we cannot live outside of society and we can live only by adapting to society. In other words, people today are by fate unable to survive if we step out of this civilized society. Therefore, civilized people can live only by adapting to society no matter what kind of society they belong to. However strict the legal laws, orders, or punishments are, humans cannot survive without obeying them. We have to follow the legal laws of the society when we commit a crime, and we have to fight in a war when it occurs. In other words, we have lost the ability to live outside of society like primitive people did, but we can live only by adapting ourselves to society. In this sense, civilized people are like livestock animals kept at a farm called society.

However, people in today's civilized society are flustered to be in the position of possibly being selected out from nature together with the whole society because this civilized society is getting incompatible with nature that is the foundation of its existence. To gain eternal existence avoiding being selected out, humans should not fight against nature, but co-exist with nature, and shift their lifestyle to adapt themselves to nature, which should have been the correct way in the first place. Of course, it is impossible for today's humans, who have made society as their own second nature and have adapted themselves to it, to adapt directly to nature at an individual level like primitive people. Then, the best way is to make society adapt to nature perfectly, and then make individuals adapt to the society, establishing the formula of "nature = society = individuals", and then the formula of "nature = individuals".

All living organisms that have physiological desires and can never create natural law. They can only survive essentially by adapting themselves to nature. Therefore, humans who shifted from being an animal of instincts to an animal living with a brain should recognize such a theory clearly and initiatively adapt themselves to nature cleverly, otherwise it is impossible to exist eternally. However, they did not have a chance to realize that under the circumstances where the actual society has become second nature satisfying their all needs, allowing them to survive with incomplete or old consciousness established around their instincts as long as they adapt themselves to society. Therefore, they are exposed to the danger of extinction together with the whole society. If they realize that and regain the true relationship with nature, as I explained earlier, they can avoid extinction, and it can be possible to exist eternally.

B. How Far Can Humans Survive by Counter-Eliminating the Natural Selection Force

Civilization and natural selection force appear as if they are inversely proportional. It also appears that the further civilization evolves, the more likely the natural selection force vanishes. However, they are not inversely proportional, nor would natural selection force vanish. The force of natural selection exists within the civilization. Therefore, today's civilization that has been developed to its highest by counter-eliminating each elimination force should have the strongest force of elimination.

Civilization is said to have been created by humans by overcoming each selection force of nature. I totally agree to that. If I can add, I would say that civilization develops higher in proportion to the level of overcoming each natural selection force. Science technology has been overcoming natural selection forces, and developing civilization proportionally. Then, will the natural selection force that has been overcome have any problem, or, will the force just vanish? No, it will not. The natural selection force that has been overcome l would appear as if it has been eliminated by humans, but in reality, they maintain their existence by turning itself into something else or transforming itself, like the law of energy. Therefore, humans have not really overcome the natural selection force, but rather, they let the force develop into a larger force of elimination along with the enhancement of civilization. Nature functions well; it will never be defeated by humans even if humans become more powerful. Nature has the system that it can complete their mission of elimination when humans can no longer adapt themselves to nature, Therefore, in nature, there is no winning by escaping like a hit-and-run accident.

The natural selection force is always stored in the population and natural environment.

Firstly, regarding population, nature in the primitive era could accommodate about 1 million people with natural food, while in civilized society, the human-made second nature, can accommodate about 3.9 billion people and is going to accommodate even more people. This population exists as a result of overcoming the natural selection force. The population over 1 million people is the population that would not have existed in natural circumstances, and indeed it is the population reached as a result that humans have overcome each force of natural selection. Therefore, population is the transformed form of natural selection force, and also a pool of the energy. This population itself will work anytime as the natural selection force that will destroy humans when they can no longer correspond with nature. Overpopulation will work as natural selection force. Here lies the danger of overpopulation. Therefore, we can say that we have to avoid population increase exceeding the food availability in each society.

Secondly, as to the natural environment, the natural ecosystem has the characteristic that can negatively change itself for humans existing in the system. Developing civilization is the process of using the convenient part of nature to create the desired environment for humans and inserting it into the natural ecosystem. In other words, developing civilization means changing the natural ecosystem endlessly, and at the same time, also creating an environment where humans as organisms cannot live in. Therefore, humans are storing the natural selection force in the natural environment as civilization develops higher. We can say that the more civilization develops, the more natural selection force is stored in the population and natural environment. Humans do not recognize this fact, enhancing civilization using the convenient elements of nature, and enhancing the selection force. In the end, nature will stand at the position where it has no other choice than eliminating humans that are unfit to nature with its general selection force.

To avoid such a nightmare to happen and let humans prosper eternally, we should learn the theory of nature, society, and human, and live wisely keeping harmony.

If we do not obtain general wisdom and keep overcoming small forces of natural selection with small wisdoms, we will eventually reach the limit of the finite earth in all aspects. Therefore, the lifestyle made by an incomplete brain will necessarily lead humans to have no other choice than giving themselves in the hand of nature in the end.

The reason that further development of today's civilization will likely cause a faster end is that the human brain is incomplete.

I may have exaggerated the natural selection force, and given you the impression that nature hates humans and wants to attack us when the chance comes, but nature does not act like that. Nature is neutral, never refuses anyone who adapts himself perfectly to nature whether he is ignorant or wise. Nature embraces such organisms forever.

Even humans can create various matters using their brain, they can never create the natural law, and also, humans can never step out of nature essentially unless they cease to be physiologic organisms. Unless they live adapting themselves to the natural law like any other animals, they can never maintain their existence as a species eternally.

C. Humans Adjusting Themselves in All Aspects to Increasing Population

All animals have a tendency to increase in number infinitely by the instinct to preserve the species. However, the possibility of infinite increase depends largely on the environment. Above all, food is the major element. As long as there is one kind of animal, humans are not an exception. They increase the population and are affected by the environment. After their appearance in Africa about 2 million years ago, humans have solved the food shortage that naturally occurred from the gradually increased population by expanding the living area and migration, but as a result of repeating such counteractions for hundreds of thousand years, humans eventually covered the earth until it became impossible to expand their living area any more. At that time, the food shortage reached its limit. It was absolute overpopulation. Then, of course, population increase stopped. Life in those times is considered to be much more severe than we can imagine, and it would have been the most difficult time in human history.

However, if the earth were larger by hundreds times than the actual size, and if it had enough food to accommodate a limitless number of people, it would be able to feed the population that keeps increasing forever. Then overpopulation would not occur and humans would have still been living a primitive life. However, the reality was harsh as I explained earlier, and the people at the end of the primitive era are considered to have lived through difficulties beyond our imagination. This pressure of overpopulation can be considered to have become stronger toward the end of the primitive era. Also, probably people in 10,000 to 20,000 years ago, the time before people shifted to the civilized era had many starvation victims, and also they had to adjust their population by killing elders and children to survive the extreme situation. What we should pay attention to was that it was the deadlock of the primitive era and at the same time it was the beginning of the shift to the civilized era. In other words, due to life under such an extreme situation, people had to make their brain work fully through the times of long and difficult life-threatening fights, recognize the various laws of nature, and apply them to grow plants and livestock animals, before they could finally produce their food by themselves. However, this process also carried a potential problem that they should not welcome the success with open arms in the long run. It was the shift only for the purpose of survival. They did not consider whether the solution along those lines would bring humans eternal prosperity. Here they already planted the seed of their future, or our today's deadlock. I ask you to remember this matter. That was the action people of those days took unconsciously for the purpose of their survival, but by that, humans shifted their stance toward nature from being controlled one-sidedly and adapting themselves to live in harmony to the stance of controlling and using nature. As a result, humans shifted from the primitive era to the civilized era.

After humans escaped from the primitive era to the civilized era and their food production became in full swing, they eventually got rid of the suffering from overpopulation, but that did not mean they had no problem to worry about. As long as humans have the tendency to increase the population infinitely due to the instinct of preservation of species like any other animals, and as long as they actually increased their population, they had to always continue their effort of securing food to feed the population. In other words, the relative overpopulation problem was never solved, but in order to eliminate the problem, they had to expand and circulate the economic activities. To explain this concretely, when a civilized society develops food productivity and gains ability to accommodate its population, that causes another overpopulation, and the increased population requires more food, a ceaseless see-saw game among population, food, and brain, where the only solution would be the ever-lasting expansion. Once the brain solved the deadlock of humans in the primitive era, it was given the role to solve human problems forever.

Let me explain in other words. All animals have the same problem of population and food. Humans evolved in the primitive era by using the brain, and when the problem of population and food reached its highest difficulty, they broke through the deadlock by producing food by themselves.

However, the problem was not completely solved. Humans put themselves in the position where they have to solve the problem of population and food by themselves forever. However, the brain that solved the problems during the first way of life has only repeated the same function to date. In other words, humans have lived to date without considering the limits of the earth, the theory of expanding circulation of population, food, and brain, as well as the evolution of the brain in a macro-perspective, nor conversing the quality of life. Therefore, because humans living by their brain are not using the brain genuinely, or due to incompleteness, humans have reached their deadlock due to the brain being contradictory.

In the primitive era, for about 1.99 million years, the population growth rate was 0.5 person a year. This was due to the strong natural selection force, such as food shortage, fierce animals, severe coldness, diseases, tropical storms, wars, etc. On the other hand, the population growth rate in 10,000 years after civilization is 390,000 per year. This was because humans have eliminated the natural selection force nearly completely. In other words, humans have produced food successfully by agriculture and farming, cured diseases by medical studies, killed fierce animals by arrows or guns, and protected themselves by wearing clothes and building houses. These eliminations of natural selection forces were not conducted for the purpose of increasing population, but as if it were the purpose, population growth accelerated its speed.

The brain was not used only for food production, but it was connected to desires that appeared along with civilization, as well as curiosity and emotions that humans inherently had. Scholarship developed arts, culture, and all possible fields. The developed results stimulated the economy, politics, food, population, brain, spirituality, among others, to develop further, and at the same time, they affected other fields mutually to urge further respective development. As times change, evolution does not require its main cause, but everything affects mutually and like a fusion chain reaction, each of them working as an element of the whole evolution. In such an interconnected relationship, civilized society gains necessity to accelerate expansion automatically and endlessly. As a result, this evolution of civilization has concurrently brought about population increase.

In history, most of the revolutions including agricultural, industrial, population, Green, scientific, etc., urged the population increase, and economic studies and social systems actively supported population increase. As a result, population on earth has grown to about 3.9 billion, growing further. This population is as a result of eliminating natural selection force for 2 million years, and it can be maintained only by further eliminating the forces. How long would that be maintained? Of course, it would not be possible forever. Instead, it has come to a deadlock today. Therefore, as I have repeatedly stated, the best way of life is to live while maintaining harmony with nature.

At the time of this writing, the world population is about 3.9 million, which is said it would exceed 7 million in 2000. Even such a topic is raised, not only politicians and scholars, but also the general public do not show so much interest in this overpopulation issue. Public opinions do not get excited to talk about it. Countries do not try to stop the increasing population, but they focus on providing daily necessities including food. However, that cannot be maintained forever. If the world population grows at the current speed, in 400 years, it will be 1 trillion, 300 times more than today. Everyone will be barely standing on earth. It is not a problem in the far future, but it is a problem currently progressing.

Therefore, while it is important to expand society as a container and enrich its quality, on the other hand, population, the items to be contained, should be strongly adjusted. It was already the time when a concrete plan to address the overpopulation issue and take strong measures.

The biggest cause of all of today's social problems is this overpopulation, which is not recognized and any countermeasures based on this issue are not applied. That is the reason for the confusion and crisis of human society. Ocean development, energy development, as well as population scattering projects by artificial satellites that are still a future dream, will all be a drop in the ocean to counter the power of population increase. Population gives us the impression that it is our good friend, but in reality, it is a devil that ruins us gradually. In today's society, atomic and hydrogen bombs, pollution, traffic accidents are the most feared issues, but in the near future, the fear of this population increase will surely be recognized as the most fearful problem in history.

Without questioning the meaning of population increase and letting it grow endlessly on this limited earth to its full capacity, we are providing necessities for living in today's development of expanding and circulation. Is that really a good idea? If we carefully listen to the bottom of history, or its essence, they will tell us the desired direction, how to steer to the direction, and everything we need.

D. Self-Operating Society

How do today's people consider and see society? Unfortunately, despite the fact that society has transformed itself to an organic, self-operating organization, people seem to consider that they have free control over society at their own will. This is a low-conscious, old-fashioned way of thinking that can be applied to simple primitive society or a society as a group. With such thinking, humans today make decisions with unrealistic ideas based on various focuses such as gods, humans, or society, within a small sphere of civilized society. As a result, humans' thinking has been separated so far from the essence or reality of society. Today's society with self-operating ability is operating itself with people steering vaguely on its back and has reached a crucial phase.

In other words, society can change itself as a self-operating entity at any time if the leash is not tight due to the theory of society. Due to not having the universal level of objectivity, humans feeling attached to society now do not know which direction that they should lead the society. Therefore, society has transformed itself naturally into a self-operating entity. Humans are buried in the society and not sure why this has happened and where they are heading to. Not only nature but also society is one entity. Without having correctly recognizing it and controlling it, humans cannot properly have control over it. I have to say that it is difficult to control it correctly with today's fiction-like thinking.

Civilized society has a current similar to the Black Current. When a boat is overthrown far off the shore in the Pacific Ocean and some of the crew catch the current to reach to an island and survived, those who know about the current in the Pacific Ocean would not be surprised, but those who don't would think the survivors swam to the island and the crew would look supermen to them. Actually, in this civilized society, there is a power of current similar to this Black Current operating.

We believe that humans have developed civilization, but this is not true. According to the necessity and currents of society, they let civilization to develop. And that was not with human plan nor by their lead. In other words, humans after civilization have only adapted themselves to this necessity, or the power of self-operation. Civilization has developed to today's state as a result. Not knowing this fact, humans believe that they created civilization and developed it by themselves. Also, they appreciated each other highly believing that they are the lord of creation. The proof that humans are only led by the necessity of civilized society is that they cannot find the direction of their civilization or the future that everyone today wants to know most. If humans created the civilization by their lead, they should know the direction or the future of the civilization as its creator. Doesn't being unable to answer mean that it is the consequence of only adjusting themselves to the necessity of civilized society, or its self-operation ability?

The reason why humans can manage society while being ignorant is that society has the self-operation ability, and what humans should do is just to grab a pole of the boat. However, it is because civilized society has this ability that humans have been buried in it to date while being ignorant and attached to it. Just like we do not feel the earth rotating while living on it, we have been attached to society without being aware of that. As Schweitzer said, humans tend to take the position of prioritizing facts over meaning, they adjust themselves to facts. However, if humans maintain their attitude of adjusting themselves to self-operating civilized society, they cannot avoid extinction. This is because the destination of the self-operating civilized society is a grave. Nothing is more terrible than ignorance. Besides, the logic is that if the current situation continues, the further science, economy, and culture continue developments, the faster the civilization reaches the limit. Therefore, humans should learn everything immediately and take the lead of civilization with their own principles.

This self-operation ability was created with the logic of expanding circulation of population, food, and brain at its core.

This ability can be created under the following preconditions.

1) The society is a social economical unit completely independent from nature and any other society.

2) A large number of unspecified free will are in effect.

3) Those who are supposed to manage the operation of society are buried in the society.

When these preconditions are satisfied, any society will obtain a self-operating ability. It can develop itself into a self-operating society. Among civilized societies, today's capitalist society is an example of such society that has satisfied the preconditions. When the theory of expanding circulation of population, food, and brain is repeatedly performed with reproductions under the said preconditions, fundamental actions of productions and consumptions repeated by humans stimulate the whole society to become a self-operating society out of necessity. We should be well aware of this.

E. Society Led by Politics

A nation, a modern management system of society, is required to manage all problems from disposing trash and excretion to welfare of people. The difficulty is beyond comparison to managing a company. Tendency is that the population keeps increasing, the economy develops, and society necessarily gets complicated. However, we can never let a society go bankrupt. Therefore, management of society should always be based on science, have leadership, be far-sighted, and be conducted under utmost caution. How about the reality? Managers who operate a company grasp the actual state of their own company scientifically and even by analyzing the social and international situation.

On the contrary, managers of society do not grasp the actual complete state of society, and never consider adapting society to natural logic. They are operating society with management sense sloppier than small business managers. Far from scrupulous leadership, their countermeasures are always late, unscientific, and complicated. If they were running a company and not a society, the organization would have gone bankrupt several times.

The reason why society is still maintained is, as I have stated repeatedly, society has a self-operation ability that automatically adjusts itself. In other words, society cannot easily go bankrupt even if it is operated poorly. If society were a company that can go bankrupt when operated poorly, various aspects of society would have been thoroughly examined and been operated with an amazing level of scientific effort.

This tells us that the undeveloped state of social science is the result of this fact. In other words, our blindness is heavily influenced by the self-operation ability of society. However, it is illogical to blame the ability of society. Rather, shouldn't we reflect on ourselves for our ignorance and stupidity that we have let society to this point without understanding the situation?

For this civilized society, wisdom is what we should depend on, but because wisdom is not dependable, we depend on politics, the second best. However, politics should be conducted based on intelligence. Under the circumstances where the intelligence that should be dependable has not been created by social science, however hard the government urges its bureaucrats to work or even they set up a special council or advisory bodies and come up with urgent measures, they can never grow out of a government that addresses problems after they occur. Social science is the brain of civilized society. Undeveloped social science means that the brain of the civilized society is not working.

Politics is often criticized, but as I explained above, politics is not to blame for everything. What is to blame is the fact that there is no logic everyone can agree on. Some may say, "Yes, there is. It's just that politics do not implement it." However, what will happen if the respective ideology that is different from person to person and that is making a vicious cycle is taken and implemented as suggested? It is plain as daylight that it will cause a huge confusion.

The problem is how to create a unified theory. Before actions are taken, unified planning and theory are necessary. Because we do not have them, reasonable politics are not conducted today, but we have no choice than letting it be. Politics of reacting after events is caused by that situation, and the politics bearing the final processing role is also caused by that situation. A unified theory should be placed before conducting politics.

When politicians deal with something related to nature, they listen to what natural scientists say relatively well. However, when it comes to society, politicians are the leaders, and social scientists are just providing referential materials or playing the role of critics. Is this because politicians have higher ability than social scientists? No, that cannot be true. A group of politicians who are not experts in sociology and most of them have just come up to the stage from nowhere cannot be more skilled than tens of thousands social scientists. Politicians are supposed to listen to social scientists about society to implement their policies. In other words, even specialized areas are different, and politicians should listen to both natural scientists and social scientists, and steer the wheel for humans without any error.

However, when it comes to society, the positions of social scientists and politicians are reversed. This is because social scientists are inferior in strength. Politicians should conduct politics based on the blueprint of human society drawn by the distinguished academic fruits of social scientists. However, social scientists have been unable to draw the unified blueprint, saying that society is too complicated to see clearly. Here occurs the reverse positions of politicians and social scientists. Therefore, this is the reason why politics cannot grow out of reacting after events or politics with no policy.

Nevertheless, politicians bear the role of steering the human society hammering out their ideas even if they don't have any, because politicians bear the final processing role like priests do.

The unsuccessfulness and vagueness of social science keeps the whole nation ignorant. Politicians chosen out of this ignorant crowd are also ignorant. Social scientists do not understand society well because society is too complicated. This is why social scientists should encourage themselves to understand society as soon as possible, enhance the intellectual level of the nation by providing reliable knowledge, and at the same time, urge politics to steer society without any error.

In any case, unless social science is developed and becomes reliable, politicians have no other way than continuing operation without any policy but adapting themselves to the self-operation ability of society, always concerned about the popularity of the nation and elections.

Essentially, civilized society is a society that should be led by intelligence. The reason why politics leads society is, partly because politics has increased its importance, but as I have explained, mainly because intelligence is lacking. Most people have not realized this inconsistency and this has become a natural norm, where politicians, scientists, and the nation have misplaced priorities. Therefore, in reality, with such norms presupposed, politicians conduct politics, social scientists play the role of critics, and the nation does not see any oddness in watching them. Still, everyone lives everyday life looking seriously.

Politicians and the nations should criticize the neglect of social scientists. Nevertheless, social scientists receive no criticism but only politicians are criticized, which is unreasonable. Besides, social scientists ignore their responsibility and leave everything to politicians, and join the nation to criticize politicians. They have misplaced their roles. Politicians believe that they are supposed to deal with everything about society, accept the criticism made by scientists as reasonable opinions, never criticizing scientists. Such politicians are self-conceited or misunderstand reality.

What actually conducts politics under the circumstance of absence of brain is the automatic adjusting self-operating ability of society. Politicians have just given their hands to the ability, and conduct politics for politicians or play politicians. Social scientists should realize their original mission as soon as possible. Then they should make the society to be led by wisdom, control the self-operation ability of society, and instruct humans to be able to live completely corresponding to the principles of nature, otherwise humans will fall in a terrible situation. All of society has become an easy, comfortable vehicle like a conveyor belt. If humans feel so comfortable that they remain on board, the society will reach the terminal station of death, involving humans with its fate. Worse still, the terminal is just around the corner.

7. Deadlock of the Second Lifestyle

A. Population Explosion

Previously I stated that the first way of life came to a deadlock because population increased to the limited availability of food on earth.

Then I also stated that the second way of life has the fate to reach a deadlock under the same theory. However, the time has already arrived. The current world population is about 3.9 billion; half of them are starving and millions of people are dying of starvation every year.

It has taken about 1.99 million years since humans appeared in an area of Africa until civilization. During that period, the population growth was about 0.5 persons a year. During 10,000 years after civilization, annual average population growth is about 390,000, which is an amazing difference. However, this is just an average; don't be surprised too early. After the industrial revolution, the population is growing at a quite rapid pace. In recent years, it is adding about 75 million persons a year. About 210,000 people are added every day around the world, totaling 75 million people a year. This abnormal population increase is called population explosion. According to some scholars, this momentum is becoming more powerful; if it continues, the population multiplication repeats in about 30 years, reaching 7 billion in 2000, 30 billion in 2070, and in 650 years later, every person will have 30 square centimeters on the surface of the earth. In 900 years, 5 people will share 30 square centimeters on all the surface of the earth from Mt. Everest to the sea. In 1,500 years, the weight of all humans will become the same weight of the earth. In 2000 years, the population will become the number that can fly to space at the same speed of the light. This is only a calculation; in reality, humans need certain space, food, clean environment, and resources. Population cannot increase like this on the earth with limited availability.

World Population Increase (AD1 to AD 2000)

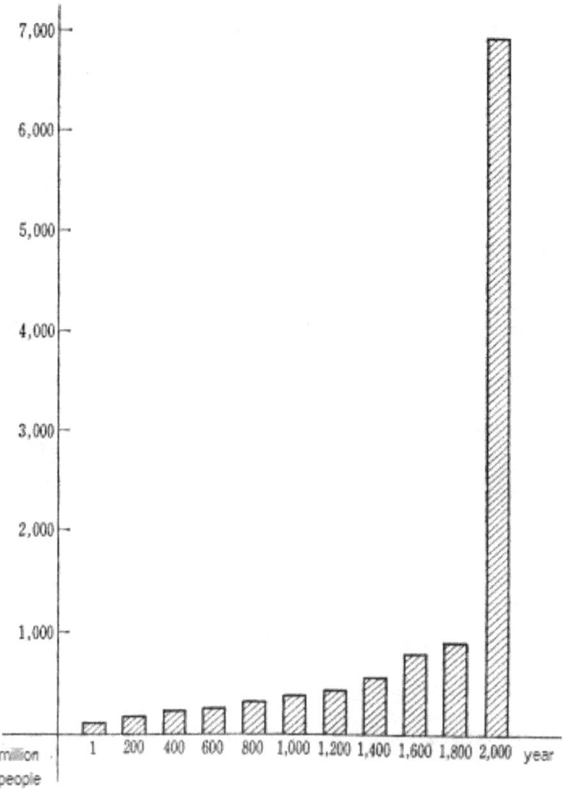

In the modern times when half of the global population is falling into starvation, the population issue is not an issue of distant future to us nor an issue in scientific fiction. It is an issue of today or tomorrow. Among the problems caused by overpopulation on the earth of limited availability, the worst of it is an issue linked to destruction of humans, such as food shortage, environmental pollution, exhaustion of resources, and overpopulation. If the number of humans continue to increase, these problems will be inevitable and destructive. Reaching such a grave time, experts and the news media have started sounding an alarm simultaneously. The United Nation's working group on population is also warning, saying "There are three elements that destroy humans; nuclear weapons, environmental pollution, and population increase. Among these, population increase has the highest possibility to be the first to destroy humans. To solve this problem, all human beings should make their best efforts."

B. Food Shortage

I explained that population and food shortage will increase in the manner like a see-saw game. The fact population has increased to the current number since civilization clearly means that food production has increased. If food production can be increased to accommodate increasing population, from the point of food availability, humans will never face any devastating problem with population. However, food production is conducted using the finite solar energy on the finite earth. Development of food production has the limit itself. Today, most countries are making great efforts in producing food to supply the increased population by using fertilizers and chemicals, as well as improving breed. However, even if we try to increase the amount of harvest per unit area, there is a limit to it. Even if we try to increase the amount of harvest by cultivating new crop fields, that is becoming difficult now, as desired new lands for agriculture are gradually disappearing, and we cannot expect great success. Even so, population remains on the rapid increase, reducing the distribution of food per person every year. Here lies the cause of a starving population increasing globally year after year. Once Malthus said, "Population will increase geometrically, but food will increase only in arithmetic progression." These words do not fit any other times than today. Various calculations are being made to find how many people can live on earth from the point of food availability, or what the capacity of the earth is. Below is one example.

Capacity of Earth from Food Availability

Food	Solar energy utilization efficiency (%)	Area needed to supply a person (cm^2)	Available population in cultivable land (3.6billion) (times)
Grain	0.05	1,200	11
Pork	0.015	4,000	3
Seaweed (mass cultivation)	12.5	5	2,530
Cows milk	0.04	1,500	8

Humans live on grain that is produced by photosynthesized solar energy, and meat that is produced with the grain. Current capacity of the earth is said to be 11 times of 3.6 billion people if we produce grains on all the cultivable areas on earth. If the grain harvested is given to livestock animals to gain meat, the capacity will be 3 times of the population. However, humans need residence, roads, factories, and other spaces to live. More population will require more space. Then the cultivable area will be less than the above, and the earth will be unable to accommodate the population shown in the chart. Besides, humans cannot survive only on grains due to nutrition issues. Overall, we can conclude that the capacity of the population is 3 times of the available pork.

However, there is another problem we have to take into our consideration. Today's agriculture largely depends on industry. Expected future lack of resources will lead industries to be dull and agriculture will have a large impact. In other words, if fertilizers, chemicals, tractors, facilities to grow vegetables, and other related necessary items for agriculture are not provided enough, production of agriculture will decrease. Produced food is often abandoned when they are considered inedible due to environmental contamination. This will continue to happen in the future. We can also expect climate change due to environmental destruction. It is said that the capacity of the earth for humans to stay eternally would be 6.4 billion as the Club of Rome announced.

C. Cause of the Deadlock of the Second Lifestyle

As I previously discussed, the universal matters from ancient times are;

(1) Humans have instincts to survive once they are born,

(2) Humans need food to survive,

(3) Humans' instinct to preserve their own species makes population increase,

(4) Brain is evolving,

(5) The size and the characteristics of the earth remain generally the same,

(6) Nature lets only organisms that adapt themselves to it survive,

(7) Human's environmental adaptation capacity has a limit, and

(8) There is a principle of population, food, and brain.

Considering that humans have existed and prospered on earth for a long period of time, we can find the fundamental and universal conditions as above.

To state reversely, the conditions above have interacted with each other and made humans prospered so far. Population increased firstly, leading to the necessity for food to provide to humans, and humans made efforts to solve food problems using the brain. This repeated cycle of actions proceeded to the infinite expanding cycle, making society grow and developed. Is this growth and development desired? Yes, on the condition that humans understand the fundamental logic of society, that humans create their own completed logic based on the logic of society, and that the growth and development are realized with humans' initiative based on that humans' logic. No, If the growth and development are realized by the logic of society under the circumstances where humans are buried in society by the logic of society, because that will lead to a deadlock and bring a tragedy, caused by an infinite development on the finite earth.

The deadlock would be inevitable. However, the faster development proceeds, the sooner it will reach a deadlock. If the current development proceeds keeping the current level, the deadlock occurred in the primitive times will occur again. Remember the great example of the end of the primitive times. You may think that our civilized era of science is different, but the consciousness and principles in the civilized era are almost the same as the primitive era. The only difference is that they were influenced by natural law and we apply natural law.

In other words, humans have lived with similar consciousness since about 2 million years ago. Without considering the meaning of increasing population or the limit and capacity of the earth, humans have lived unthinkingly. Civilized society was not created from the lessons learned at the deadlock of the primitive era but it was created by the efforts of survival instinct discovering a new way of life and succeeding in survival. Discussions aside, in reality, our society is developing faster, gaining its speed, and at the same time, it is going into the deadlock at the same speed. That is the same principle of the situation at the end of the primitive era. Reasonably enough, the principle of population increase is the same, complication of human society does not change its essential quality. The situation of the end of the primitive era is just being repeated as history repeats itself. There is no wonder to this phenomenon.

D. The Second Deadlock

In the first lifestyle, humans lived sparsely on the finite earth, while in the second lifestyle, humans live thickly on the same finite earth. The difference between these two lifestyles is whether people cover the earth thinly or thickly, but what is common to both is the principle of expanding circulation of population, food, and brain. Just like the first lifestyle reached a deadlock by this principle, it is inevitable that the second lifestyle will reach the deadlock eventually.

The real second deadlock will arrive soon. When it comes, humans will fall in a devastating situation. Even at the first deadlock, which was a simple deadlock when the population exceeded food availability, the situation was so severe as I described previously. The second deadlock will not be a simple one caused by just the food availability, but by various other elements mixed together. In today's society, the second way of life, the industrial economy has developed as if it has covered the agricultural economy, presenting the industrialized society. However, as the earth has limits in many aspects, this grand development of industrialized society will eventually reach the various finites of the earth. The consequences will not be simple as the first deadlock when the food shortage restricted population, but will be a devastating deadlock caused by overall natural selection force causing population significantly reduced. Industrialized society is a complicated and diversified society expanded by the logic of economy and operated by general marketability or principles of society.

The grand development of industry after the industrial revolution is making various harmful substances released in the air, water, and land, changing the natural environment and exceeding the acceptance range of the internal environment of humans. Industrialization is a means for humans to live better. However, ignorant humans have focused on this means and are destroying their aim which is maintaining their survival. Infinite expansion of industrialization in the finite ecosystem of the earth will surely cause mass mortality eventually. This is the general deadlock of the second lifestyle.

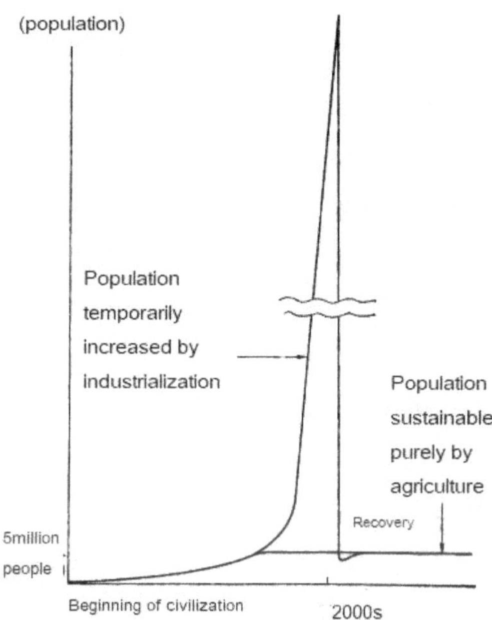

Also, from the view of resources, humans are under very severe conditions. Industry has been supported by various resources from the earth. These resources have been stored in the earth for billions of years; therefore, they are like a finite legacy passed down from our ancestors. Thanks to the industrialized economy based on these resources, several times more population have survived than the estimated number of population sustained purely by the agricultural economy. However, when these resources start to run out one after another in the near future, industry cannot avoid going downward. In other words, the temporal industrialized society that has depended on these finite resources from the start will realize a grand development to its peak, and after that, along with the drastic decrease of resources, it will only make a sharp curb downward. If that happens, the population that has increased with the legacy passed down from the ancestors will also decrease rapidly as shown in the chart.

We can say that the characteristic of the second society is like a castle on sand or one night's dream from the start.

Reduction in agricultural production is also inevitable. Agriculture in the industrial economy has increased productivity amazingly blessed with various machineries, fertilizers, chemicals, facilities, cars, and communication tools. This is why Malthus's prediction seemed to have failed. This high productivity of agriculture will only fall rapidly with the decrease of industry. Here we can predict a rapid decrease in population from the point of resources. In other words, we can say that population will be decreased to the level that can keep the balance with the decreased agriculture. In this way, the second deadlock is explicable even only from the aspect of resources.

Therefore, the state of the second deadlock will be quite different from the first deadlock. If we call the first deadlock caused by food shortage a dreadful state, we should call the second deadlock a hell, a devastating state caused by various elements of natural selection forces on earth. As British journalist G. R. Taylor wrote in his book "The doomsday book; can the world survive?", demographers say that population continues to increase at the current ratio, and it will reach 25 billion in 2070, and then decrease rapidly to 2 billion. "The Limits to Growth" by the Club of Rome also says that if population and industry continue to develop with the current speed, population will drastically decrease in the 2010s. Hellish situations cannot be avoided. I may repeat the same topic but I would like to present what can happen.

Even when I discuss imaginary situations, I cannot ignore the population issue that is the basic issue of society. Population and society are to be treated as equal. Population increased slowly in the past, but it is gaining its speed recently, going to multiply in roughly 30 years. Humans were born on this earth and can live only on this earth. This our mother earth has hardly changed and remained about the same size. On this finite earth, only humans are multiplying in number. It is truly clear that the earth will be eventually full of humans.

When animals are forced to live in a small space with many other fellows, they feel stressed and possibly go extinct, as above-mentioned Taylor and an American biologist say supported by animal experiments. Even if we ignore the destruction caused by stress, population of several times more than current number on this small earth, vital elements for humans such as air, water, land, space, resources, and food will surely run out. I don't think I have to say the fate of humans.

Also, the amazing development of modern scientific technology shifted the slow-paced, agricultural human society to today's fast-paced, complicated industrial society. Its scientific technology and industrialization spurred population increase while causing pollution in wide areas to precious materials such as air, water, land, and food, that are becoming less available due to increased population, pouring salt of chemicals on a wound. Also, the large scale industrialization and unplanned grand development of natural areas are destroying the ecosystem on earth, making it impossible for all organisms including humans to survive.

If humans continue their current lifestyle, they will have to face a devastating situation in the not so distant future. If that happens, human society will become a hell beyond our imagination, beyond comparison to the dismal state of any natural disasters or wars. Real horror is the fact that it is an inevitable human-generated calamity that will attack us very slowly as if it struggle us with floss silk if humans continue the current lifestyle. Most people today fear of pollution and wars, but in the near future, they will realize that population increase will cause extinction of humans.

Also, this will be the worst terror in history and society will be thrown into an uproar. We must not misunderstand that the devastation will be still later on, but the floss silk has already started to strangling our neck. It is our problem not future generations, a reality we cannot just look at it as bystanders.

If it becomes an issue of uproar, politicians and scientists will gather all their strength even in turmoil to counter the terror by implementing birth control at global level, revolutionary food production, living under the sea, living in the air using satellites, or by developing other technologies we cannot imagine today.

However, we have too short time and too limited wisdom to do so to avoid the crisis forever. What humans can do is to delay the crisis by some decades or longer, or to implement a way to avoid humans going extinct all at once.

Today's deadlock is, as I have repeated to state, the second deadlock. There are two reasons why no one has realized it is the second deadlock.

The first reason is that there is no record of the first deadlock. If human brain and culture had been developed by the end of the first way of life, they must have made some kind of records that the increased population caused shortage of natural food reaching a deadlock, and that they expected out of the crisis by shifting to the second lifestyle using their evolved brain. However, the human brain had not developed to that level at that time leaving no record, making it difficult for us to recognize today's deadlock as the second one.

I would like to tell you the second reason. If philosophers, historians, economists, and sociologists had studied human society logically from the deepest foundation, not just phenomenal aspects, they should have realized the second deadlock, but they haven't. Most scholars considered primitive society only as an animalistic society or society of economics with collecting from nature, and also thought the reason why civilized society started was that humans had free hands and feet, as well as good brains, without giving it deeper consideration. In other words, they haven't considered what drove civilized society formed and developed. They have considered the population unilaterally. Here lies the second reason.

I believe that from the reasons above, today's deadlock has not been recognized as the second deadlock for humans.

E. Essence of the Second Deadlock

The danger of destruction of all mankind has occurred from the food shortage that has been caused by environmental contamination and increased population. Environmental contamination has been caused by expansion of the industrial economy grown beyond the ecosystem of the earth, and the expansion of the industrial economy attributed to increased population and increased desires of the population. To state reversely, even if industrialization did not happen and it did not cause environmental contamination, if rapid population increase exceeds food availability, that only can cause the danger of destruction of humans.

Furthermore, if industrialization occurs, as did in reality, that adds environmental contamination, that will be an extra cause of the danger. However, rather than the danger from the food shortage caused by increased population, when too rapid industrialization beyond the limit of ecosystem occurs causing environmental contamination, the danger from contamination attracts more attention, making the danger from food shortage seem less significant. Today's danger happened to have been caused by these two causes, and this is why the situation is complicated. However, we should not misplace the priorities. The danger is primarily caused from food shortage caused by increased population, and the danger caused by industrialization or environmental contamination is secondary. To explain this more concretely, the second lifestyle is the way to live thickly covering the earth, but this thickness has its limit, and population alone would cause the second deadlock. Industrialization just spurred the process. The primary cause of the deadlock is food shortage, and industrialization is secondly. Therefore, even if reality looks the opposite, we should not misunderstand.

Now, I would like to explain this second deadlock from the side of nature, our life's foundation.

8. Characteristics of Nature

As was in the first time, the problem of this deadlock is related to the characteristics of nature. Therefore, we have to understand them carefully. As we look closely, nature has the characteristics of finiteness, stability, harmony, and balance. It is not unchanging, but it is also evolving or changing in a long run, and the axis of coordinates of finiteness, stability, harmony, and balance are slightly changing. Living organisms are evolving themselves to adapt to nature to be harmonized with nature.

I believe this is the way and characteristics of nature. However, it also has the characteristics that it changes itself drastically and evolutions of living organisms cannot catch up with it shifting the axis of coordinates greatly. However, nature hardly causes such a state as it can evolve only slightly. This is why orgasms have survived on earth since its birth for more than 3 billion years without incessantly, and millions of species flourish on today's earth. However, today, humans, one species of the living organisms, are changing the axis of coordinates of nature greatly and changing the characteristics of nature to the state that life cannot exist in it. This is because humans have become the main force on earth and formed a society of ceaselessly developing industrial economy there.

I have presented the conclusion first, but I would like to discuss in detail logically. Firstly, I will present problems of finiteness, stability, harmony, and balance of nature occurring under the "stable nature". Secondly, I will present the nature that has shifted the axis of coordinates under "unstable nature". Lastly, I will present the conditions on the side of humans and conclude under "humans as living organisms".

A. Stable Nature

Since American Professor Kenneth E. Boulding said the earth is finite and should be considered as Spaceship Earth, the recognition that the earth is finite has spread. The earth is finite not in size but also in lifespan, resources, amount of solar energy it accepts, and the ability to produce plants. Therefore, I am going to discuss these one by one, and then the characteristics of nature such as finiteness, stability, harmony, and balance. These characteristics of stability and balance are all seen in earth's ecological system. I will discuss them in the section of the system.

1. Lifespan of the Earth

The earth was born in the space environment and is one of the members that form the space environment. It was born as a burning mushy lump of simple material 4.5 billion years ago.

After that, with the deep love of mother universe and its own growing force, it developed itself transforming simple materials through various processes. It is said that the lifespan of the earth is 9 billion years, so it has just reached the turning point, having another 4.5 billion years to live. It is also said that the earth will end as the sun grows gradually into a giant planet and engulf the earth. However, even though earth's lifespan is finite, living organisms on earth will be able to stay more than 3 billion years of the remaining 4.5 billion years, as they have for more than 3 billion years of the past 4.5 billion years. Then humans should be able to stay on earth for another billions of years if they adapt themselves to the earth well.

2. Size of the Earth

In ancient times, people thought the earth had no limit, but gradually they came to understand the earth is round and finite. No one today doubts that because it was confirmed by the images sent from Apollo space missions and we can also see the earth from the sky when we fly. The earth is about 13,000 kilometers in diameter, 600 million square meters on the surface, one third of which is land and the rest is the sea. The earth is literally finite.

3. Resources

Resources are the substances that are the base of production activities. The development of scientific technology is changing substances we had not seen into resources. This fact makes us think we can change every substance into resources, and that is true. However, in reality, only substances that can be applied to developed scientific technology are called resources. Resources are the property of the earth stored in billions of years. They can be used up someday, so they are finite.

4. Receivable Solar Energy

According to "Warnings to Humans" by Sha Seiki, the solar energy the earth receives in one year is 5 x 1023 calories. The author explains the basis of this calculation as follows; according to the observation of satellites, a flat placed vertically to sunbeam in outer space can receive energy of 2 calories per minute per square centimeter. However, half of the energy is consumed while the sunbeam goes through the atmospheric layer, and only 1 calorie can reach the surface of the earth. However, half of the energy is reflected and sent back from the earth to space. The actual usable energy received on the earth surface vertical to sunbeam is 0.5 calories per minute per square centimeter.

Then, how much solar energy can the entire surface of the earth absorb? The surface that is vertical to sunbeam is extremely limited, and also, half of the surface is in nighttime while the other is in daytime. This means the surface that can receive the sunbeam vertically is only one fourth of the whole surface. The solar energy received on earth will be 0.1 calorie per minute per square meter on average, or 0.15 calories at most.

The surface of earth is 600 million square kilometers, or 6 x 1018 square centimeters. As a yearly unit is more convenient for a general view. A year is 525,600 minutes. One square centimeter absorbs 0.15 calories per minute. The solar energy the earth receives yearly is 5 x

1023 calories. Probably not many of you will understand this immediately, but I am sure you understand that the solar energy received is also limited.

5. Plant Production Ability of the Earth

Green plants are the source of life for all animals. As everyone knows, plants grow on solar energy. However, the amount of solar energy received on the earth and the land are both limited. Therefore, plant production ability is finite. I already mentioned this matter in the food shortage of the second deadlock.

6. Ecosystem of the Earth

Circulation of water and air, heat balance, natural depuration, balance of living organisms forms the ecosystem of the earth, and they interconnect mutually and inseparably, therefore I would like to discuss as a whole here. Since before life appeared on earth, water, air, and other substances had kept balanced circulation and formed the environment as if it is one giant thread. Animals including humans appeared there, making a more complicated ecosystem. What we call the natural environment today is this ecosystem.

There are several ways to explain the ecosystem, but I believe the following explanation would be easy to understand. Think of natural small birds. It is very rare for a small bird to live alone but they often make a flock connected in various ways. Besides, other animals and plants exist around them in bigger connection circles. This means that these small birds are members of a group of larger connection circles of organisms. This group of organisms are not independent. They exist in deep connection with the inanimate environment such as the sun, air, water, and land. They all exist connected mutually in a coordinated relationship as a whole. They are connected to each other as if an invisible thread is connecting them. This coordination of the whole is called an ecosystem.

Let us think about each element that forms the ecosystem. Firstly, we will look at the inanimate environment.

(a) Water Circulation

Water circulation is a repetition of movement of water of the sea and the land, evaporating with solar energy, changing itself to a cloud, then to rain that goes back to the sea and the land.

(b) Air Circulation

There is a balance of radiant heat between the sun and the earth. This balance has differences depending on the latitudes, causing air to circulate. This is also the cause of wind and seasons.

(c) Heat Balance

Solar heat gives warmth to the earth, but if the earth surface is bare, the average temperature would be -23 degrees centigrade. The earth has kept its temperature at about 14 degrees centigrade because the vapor and carbon dioxide gas keep the heat on the earth as if they are clothing to the earth, preventing heat from escaping into space, which is called the greenhouse effect. There is a law in the ecosystem that the higher the earth's temperature goes, more vapor and carbon dioxide gas from the sea occur, increasing the greenhouse gas effect and heating the earth, but on the other hand, the lower it goes, the less vapor and carbon dioxide gas occur, decreasing the greenhouse effect and cooling the earth. Therefore, if it had been a wall between the equator and the polar areas to prevent the exchange of heat, the sea water near the equator would be boiling hot sending up a large among of vapor and carbon dioxide gas in the air making the equator an inferno, while the polar regions would be the regions of death with temperatures far below zero.

If this occurred in reality, there would be no living organisms on earth. There is no wall between the equator and polar areas. The sea water circulates actively due to the difference in temperature, or heat exchanging. It carries heat without freezing all around the year, and controls the greenhouse effect to be appropriate, making the earth a comfortable habitat for living organisms. The earth is a natural air conditioner equipped with a thermostat. The balance of the inanimate environment of the ecosystem is amazing.

I will come back to inanimate environment later, and now I would like to discuss the ecosystem.

(d) Food Chain

The most basic relationship in the environment of the ecosystem is the food chain. Living organisms are in the relationship of to eat and to be eaten. In this relationship, firstly, the producer, or green plants, create organic substances by photosynthesis using the chemical energy of the sun. The primary consumers, or animals, eat them. Then the secondary consumer animals eat them, and the third consumer animals eat the secondary consumers. However, they are not the last ones to consume, but after plants and animals die, bacteria and fungi decompose them into the source of plants. The plants are eaten by animals, making a cycle of food. This looks as if the whole world of living organisms is connected by a chain of food, and this is why this relationship is called a food chain.

As above, all living things on earth are mutually related. In other words, all of them cannot survive without depending on other life including bacteria and fungus. This food chain shows the circulation of energy and purification of life, and balance among life, and other delicate natural phenomena.

(e) Energy Circulation of Living Organisms

Plants store the solar energy by photosynthesis. Animals eat the plants taking in the energy. When they die, the bodies are decomposed creating nitrate nitrogen, which become the source of plants. Energy is circulating like this, but the amount decreases as it is released out when it is passed down. However, by supplying the lacking energy from the sun, the balance of living organisms is maintained, as well as the balance with their outer world.

(f) Self-Purification of Nature

The earth is maintained and purified by decomposers. Animals discharge excrements during their life, and their body after death, to the earth. Plants also discharge their dead body to the earth. If there had been no decomposers to decompose the dead bodies since the appearance of life on earth until today, the surface of the earth would have been covered by excrement and dead bodies of animals and plants. Fortunately, the earth has decomposers who keep working on decomposing excrement and dead bodies and purifying nature. This has kept water, air, and land clean on earth, and is one of the systematic phenomena of the food chain.

(g) Balance among Living Organisms

The steady power balance of animal and plant species are generally maintained in the relationship of eating and being eaten. Even when one species increases abnormally in number temporarily, natural control force regains the original condition or close enough to keep the overall balance. I would like to present an example biologists give when they talk about the balance of living organisms.

On an about 3,000 square kilometer grass land of Kaibab Plateau in the northern Arizona of the U.S., there were about 4,000 dears in

1905. However, the grass land was supposed to accommodate about 30,000 deer. People decided that there were only 4,000 deer because carnivorous animals were eating deer, and for several years they repeated large-scale hunting and killed more than 700 pumas and more than 7,000 coyotes. As a result, deer increased its population to more than 40,000 in 1918, reaching 100,000 in 1923. However, this population of 100,000 exceeded the capacity of the grassland. Within two years, the balance collapsed altogether, leading 60,000 deer starved to death, and kept decreasing in number. Only 10,000 deer had survived in 1929. This is an example of a natural control force; deer increased its number because there were no predators for them, but their population was adjusted by another force. Another force in this case was the restraint force occurred from the overpopulation against food plants. The fact that the population increased to 100,000 in 1923 means that the grass land had the capacity, even if not plenty, for nearly 100,000 deer. Therefore, with our common sense, we can guess that the grass land could feed 70,000 to 80,000 deer at least. The reality, however, was that the population rapidly dropped to 10,000. We can consider easily that this may be due to diseases from congestion, or the overcrowded deer treading on the grass blocking it to grow severely, but I am confident that it was the result of power balance among the deer.

When the population of deer started to increase over the capacity of the grassland, the land should have been almost bare. Then the food for the deer would be new sprouts only. However, the growth of sprouts is very slow, and feeding ability is small. We can imagine that it was impossible to feed 100,000 deer and they died of starvation one after another. Survived deer kept eating new sprouts, making a vicious cycle and decreasing the population to 10,000, a population that new spouts could feed. I have described the event as if I observed it, but I know a similar story about a person called Mr. A who kept piglets, not deer.

It was in mid-April of more than 10 years ago. Mr. A heard from someone that pigs could grow on grass only, and put more than 20 piglets to pasture on 2 hectares of grassland in a mountain 5 kilometers away from his residence. The piglets grew healthy on grass at first. However, it was too early in the season for sprouts to grow and the grass was less than 5 centimeters tall. The food ran out for piglets in only one week, so piglets started to dig soft land for clover roots. Mr. A had soon realized that it was too early for grass to grow before letting piglets on the land, but thought that it was already getting warmer, the grass would grow rapidly, and grass would soon overgrow the needs of the piglets, so decided to supply other food until the grass caught up.

However, after 10 days, then 20 days, the land did not recover their grass. Grass on other fields had already grown more than 20 centimeters, long enough to be blown by wind. Mr. A admitted that it was completely his mistake, but as he had started his pasture against his family stopping him, he could not easily give it up and lose his face.

Eventually, he found an excuse for himself that he was just giving a playground for the piglets and decided he would just give up the pasture, and kept the land with piglets as it was for more than two months. During that time, piglets dug and ate up all the clover roots they love, and all the skins of about 100 Italian poplars of 10 centimeters in diameter to the height they could reach and let the trees die. They ate their favorite kinds of grass and left the grass they didn't like.

On the 2 hectares grassland, unhealthy, unappetizing looking grass had grown sparsely blown by the wind. Even the stubborn Mr. A was surprised by the force of nature and ended keeping piglets on the pasture after three months. The lovely piglets of 2kg each before letting on the pasture became skinny, less than 15kg (they were supposed to be more than 50kg) with long grown hair, rounded back, very agile. They somewhat looked like boars, giving us the impression of funny and sadness at the same time. They fell into such a state even Mr. A added food every day. If he didn't, most of them would have died of hunger.

I wrote about the relationship between deer and the grass land that was losing its feeding capacity logically through the experience of my friend Mr. A. However, these events happened because humans simplified nature and tried to gain the results in a short time. The complicated and eternally continuing natural world, such extreme phenomena hardly occur but nature maintains its balance.

Population at the first deadlock and population in Japan during its isolation period did not fall dramatically, but they were maintained to a certain number. Lions on the fields of Africa, and deer in Mt. Kinka (an island east to Oshika Peninsula of Miyagi Prefecture, 6km from north to south, 4km from east to west) have both reached to the maximum of the capacity, and also no natural enemy for them on their territories, but they have never changed their population drastically but they maintain their population at certain number for a long time. These are because the good balance of the population and the food produced on respective lands have been maintained. The populations at the first deadlock and the Japanese population during the isolation era must have been in a good balance with the food produced from the roots, stems, and seeds of plants, and the number of animal babies born every year. Deer on Mt. Kinka had been maintained at roughly 500 for hundreds of years, but since about 10 years ago, when humans started to give extra food seeing them in food shortage in winter, deer population has grown about 600 breaking the balance of food production on the island. Besides the variety of grasses, there are many trees on Mt. Kinka. The trees are in danger because of the increased 600 deer on the island. This means the deer, too, will face danger.

Lions in Africa are in good balance with the number of other animals like zebras and buffalos that grow on grass. Therefore, deer in the U.S. regained the balance when they reduced their population to 10,000. Even after the grassland recovers and the capacity is returned, in the long run, deer will not be able to exceed the capacity. In this way, the balance among the living organisms are perfectly maintained in the relationship of the ones that eat and the ones that are eaten.

My explanations about balance among living organisms have become long and the whole explanation have also become long, so I would like to round up what I have explained. The earth had been a large form with good balance where substances circulate since before life occurred. There life appeared and made a natural environment called an ecosystem. All the elements in the ecosystem keep good balance with each other deeply connected with each other. Non-life environments such as water and air circulation and heat balance are maintained by the delicate relationship among the sun, the sea, land, air, and space. The fundamental relationship of the life environment is the food chain. Through this food chain, life energy circulation, natural purification, and balance between organisms maintain perfect balance.

As we can understand from above, nature is a well-organized system, and a unified form with stability, harmony, and balance. Living organisms are let live by such nature, and they can live eternally only under such nature. However, there is an organism that is drastically changing the stability, harmony, and balance of nature. Needless to say, that is us, humans. Next, we would like to see the changing characteristics of nature.

B. Nature Becoming Unstable

The reason humans are changing the stable, balanced nature into undesired, unstable nature is because, as I have explained, the population that has filled the capacity of the closed space on earth has started to live on agriculture and also on industrialization by building factories one after another to satisfy the diversified desires. In other words, 3.9 billion of humans are pushing forward the industrialization on the limited space of the earth ignoring the possibility that only agricultural life may break the systems of food chain, natural self-purification, and balance among organisms, by changing the environment into uninhabitable state for organisms through contaminating water, air, and soil. This destruction of nature is reported by mass media every day, so everyone knows about this fact. This destruction of nature has changed the characteristics of nature drastically. Let us now look at them. I would like to explain in the order of water contamination, unbalanced heat, concentration caused by food chain, natural non-purification, unbalance among organisms, and soil contamination.

(a) Water Contamination

Water in the natural environment before being interrupted by the human environment got contaminated by natural disasters like flood and volcanic eruptions, or contaminated by animals or plants, but nature's self-purification system always purified itself, therefore there was no accumulated contamination. However, since the human environment joined the natural environment, water was only to be contaminated by wastewater from homes, factories, mining, agriculture and fishing. To list the worst contaminants, they are detergents, plastic products, agricultural chemicals, cyanide, mercury, lead, cadmium, PCB, ABS, radioactive substances, waste oil, and sludge, among others.

As a result, rivers, lakes, and the sea have all been contaminated, even making people who ate the fish from there suffered and died from Itai-itai disease. Furthermore, generated red tide gave a huge impact on fishery, oil film that covered the sea blocked sea from evaporating affecting the water circulation causing extraordinary weather. We cannot ignore contaminated drinking water. Like this, water contamination has affected the characteristics of the earth making it a big issue.

(b) Air Pollution

As with the water contamination, air has been polluted endlessly since human environment joined the natural environment causing a serious problem. Sources of pollution are households, thermal power stations, air-conditioned buildings, factory boilers and furnaces, heavy chemical industry complex, vehicles, garbage incinerators, and airplanes, and primary contaminants are sulfur oxide (transformed into sulfurous acid), nitric oxide, air borne dust, soot, carbon monoxide, lead, nitric monoxide, hydrocarbon, nitrogen dioxide. If we include substances of ultrarace level, there are hundreds of contaminants, and most of them are said to be generated from burned petroleum.

They affect the human body slowly but directly. Repeated exposure to sulfurous acid gas causes mucosal tissues such as bronchus and lungs chronic inflammation, further causing rhinitis, laryngitis, bronchitis, asthma, or emphysema. Also, these substances cause synergism in nature and generate oxidants, sulfuric acid, nitric acid, or other more heavily poisonous substances. Recent sulfuric or nitric acid rain proves this fact. The atmosphere for human society has changed from the original atmosphere of the earth to be poisonous. Life requiring a gas mask is expected in big cities in the near future.

(c) Unbalanced Heat

Please remember that, in the section of "heat balance", I explained the reason why the earth temperature is maintained at about 14 degrees centigrade is because water vapor and carbon dioxide cover the earth preventing heat from escaping from the earth to space as greenhouse effect, and at the same time, this heat balance greatly affects the sea positively. As the sea is contaminated to be covered on its surface, vapor and carbon dioxide are not exchanged smoothly making temperature adjustment dysfunction. At the same time, water circulation does not occur. Climate change is thought to occur as a result.

Also, exceeding carbon dioxide in the air due to industrialization and other factors causes climate change. Carbon dioxide absorbs a great amount of radiant heat; as more carbon dioxide is generated, it heats up the earth. When the radiant heat from the sun and the radiant heat escaping from the earth into space is balanced, the average temperature remains the same, but more carbon dioxide breaks this balance and heats up the earth eventually. Carbon dioxide generated when oil and coals are burned is only on the increase. The sea absorbs the carbon dioxide to keep the balance, but this absorption takes some time. Therefore, when carbon dioxide is released by industry or other factors more than this absorption ability, the adjustment of temperature does not catch up. It can be assumed that the earth will become a boiling hell. Furthermore, if the earth is heated, ice in both polar areas will melt, reducing the land by some percentages.

On the contrary, however, it is said that the earth is getting colder. Many people think that, along with carbon dioxide, more air contaminants are released, blocking the sunlight, reducing the solar energy received on the earth surface, lowering the temperature. This is considered to be a graver phenomenon than global warming, because that would reduce agricultural productivity. In any case, water and air contamination will surely change the natural system gravely.

(d) Concentration by Food Chain

All living organisms are connected in the food chain. This great system is at the same time the cause of today's danger. According to the previously introduced "Warnings to Humans", when water is contaminated, firstly planktons and small fish that eat contaminated soil at the bottom of water absorbs poisonous substances such as mercury. Plankton and small fish are eaten by larger fish, which are eaten by even larger fish, concentrating the mercury. Food chain concentrates the poisonous substances. When they reach human bodies, they are significantly concentrated. Even though the contaminants are only a small amount at first, they are considerably concentrated by the time they reach humans. Minamata disease and Itai-itai disease were caused by this logic. This concentration by food chain occurs also in soil contamination by agricultural chemicals.

Recently, BHC were found to be contained in cow milk and also in human milk, and caused a large fuss in the world. This is another case of concentration. BHC in the soil went through rice straw into milk cow and concentrated. Not just in rice straw but in rice BHC is concentrated. It directly comes into our body to be stored. Cadmium contamination occurs in the same process. I say that the food chain is the cause of the danger, but nature is only working according to its principles. We should know that the real cause is us humans.

(d) Natural Non-Purification

In natural water, air, and soil, there are various decomposers like mold, bacteria, and microorganisms in small animals. Until recently, these decomposers have maintained nature purified and uncontaminated, but since the time population filled the earth, humans have abandoned various wastes to nature exceeding the capacity of nature's purification ability, contaminating water, air, and soil, or the entire earth. Among the wastes were plastic products that had not existed in nature, or that cannot be decomposed by bacteria. Plastic products generate poisonous gas when burned, and remain undecomposed when buried in the soil. This will add another factor of contamination to the earth. This impurification of the earth is a grave problem causing human health problems and climate change.

(f) Unbalance Among Organisms

Modern civilization process looks like it is keeping only desired organisms alive and killing all other undesired organisms to let only humans survive. It seems like replacing the natural environment with an artificial environment, as if humans are making the earth machinery or a spaceship. However, as I discussed in the sections of the food chain and the balance among organisms, all living organisms are in the relationship of depending mutually. Even some organisms seem unwanted by humans, in many cases they play important roles as natural enemies, cleaners, or fertilizers. What will happen if we cut the diversified natural chain into pieces and establish a simple layer only? The most terrible result will be the rapid decrease of humans who are the top of the organisms and implementing such processes.

Population has increased in recent years. To let the whole population survive, simplifying nature to some extent is inevitable. However, we should not just simplify it without consideration, we should listen to nature and make reasonable simplifications.

(g) Soil Contamination

Everyone would imagine agriculture when they hear the word soil. Agriculture and soil are deeply related. Agriculture is the source of our life, and nothing is more important. If soil, the foundation of agriculture, is contaminated, that is a grave problem, because it is a problem that directly affects our health and life. However, humans contaminate this very soil. The contamination of soil is rapidly progressing by the poisonous substances from waste water from mining and factories, as well as residual or stored agricultural chemicals, and sulfurous acid gas and cadmium emitted from factory smokestacks.

The primary soil contaminants are agricultural chemicals. After World War II, Japanese agriculture produced new plant varieties that can be grown with agrochemicals and chemical fertilizers. Therefore, the amount of agrochemicals used has become large, and a part of that is stored in the human body through food chain, causing various problems. On the other hand, the more they are used, the more resistant harmful insects become, and increase in number. Like a see-saw game, chemicals used are becoming stronger. After unwanted natural enemies have died, humans have to pollinate apple flowers which used to be the task of insects. Furthermore, agricultural chemicals are killing all the decomposers in soil that live by millions in one square meters bearing important roles, producing dead land. This is said to bring about a decrease in production in the near future.

Where are humans heading by harming nature like this? I would like to stop my explanation here, about nature that has shifted its coordinate axis due to instability, disharmony, and imbalance.

C. Humans as Living Organisms

We have seen the characteristics of nature, which is the foundation of human existence. As a result, we have found that stable nature will let organisms live eternally, but unstable nature, or nature that shifts its coordinate axis, does not guarantee the survival of organisms. This is because organisms have an internal environment similar to earth's ecosystem, and at the same time, humans' evolution speed is generally at a fixed pace and cannot catch up with rapid change of nature. Therefore, I would like to discuss evolution and the internal environment in this section. By doing so, we can understand what is required of humans to adapt themselves to the natural environment, and ultimately, the desired relationship between the earth and humans.

Some 4.5 billion years have already passed since the birth of the earth. It evolved from the state of burning hell to the current state. In the course of the process, it has generated various types of organisms according to the environment of the time. Natural environment keeps evolving, even though the pace is very slow. Long years have brought about great results. One example is that the air now consists of one third of oxygen and 0.38% of carbon dioxide, while there was no oxygen and 91% was carbon dioxide when the earth was born. However, the offspring of the organisms generated billions or tens of billions of years ago, according to the environment at that time, still exist. Even though they are the offspring, not the original forms, the reason that organisms can exist in the greatly changed environment is because they have transformed themselves to adapt to the change of nature and maintained balance.

In other words, they adapted themselves by evolving themselves. As a result, for today's organisms, offspring of ancient organisms, today's air composition is the most suitable for them, and they cannot survive in the air their ancestors lived in.

Evolution of the earth is very slow. As such, organisms born on the earth can evolve only slowly and in a similar manner.

The bodies of organisms generated during the process of such evolution are said to be very similar to the ecosystem of the earth like a photocopy. However, the mother nature of the earth can exist without organisms, but organisms as its children cannot live without the nature of the earth. Besides, it is not that just staying with the nature allow them to live, but they can survive only adapting their internal environment to natural environment. So far, they have been evolving slowly to the pace of the slow evolving earth in an equestrian-like manner, not causing any serious issues. However, when the human environment joined, the earth's nature started to change drastically, and organisms could not catch up with the change anymore, because there is a limit to internal environmental adaption ability to the natural environment. When the earth's nature changes beyond this limit, organisms have to cease their existence. Of course the adaptation range depends on individuals or species. However, the range does not differ so greatly. At the same time, such organisms exist in the relationship of serving each other in the food chain. From the aspect of existence, under ceaseless change of nature, they have no choice than extinct one after another.

As organisms have such an evolution process and a limit of internal environment, we should not let nature continue in an unstable state that exceeds the evolution speed and internal environmental capacity. In other words, nature has the characteristic of changing itself forever, and it will keep its existence even if humans apply changes to nature. The problem is that organisms will not be able to survive there anymore. Therefore, we should stop the change of nature and the shift of its coordinate axis, because we have come to the limit.

Now, let us see things reversely. Organisms with physiologic features cannot follow nature by transforming themselves forever. Inconveniently for them, nature has the characteristic of changing only for the worse endlessly. If nature did not have this characteristic of changing only for the worse, environmental destruction and pollution would never have occurred and organisms would never have gone extinct. For organisms, this characteristic of nature is very inconvenient. Furthermore, humans actively affect this characteristic of nature out of necessity of evolution of civilized society, and have changed it in reality, destroying the conditions of survival of organisms. Even nature has such a characteristic of changing, if humans do not affect it, nature would not change as if it had no such characteristic. Therefore, humans are the ones who affect such characteristics of nature out of necessity of evolution of civilized society and indeed affecting the causes of danger we face today.

Here I would like to present the conclusion of "Characteristic of Nature". Nature has the characteristic of changing itself infinitely, while organisms cannot catch up with the changes forever. Herein lies the problem, and herein lies the condition for destruction. However, nature does not change rapidly by itself alone. If it is not forced to change by humans, nature will maintain a stable condition and let organisms live forever. Humans cannot grow out of organisms no matter how hard they use scientific technology, and they cannot create laws. Therefore, as all other organisms do not, humans should not harm nature anymore, but maintain natural lifestyles as much as possible, and take the initiative to adapt themselves to nature to stay on earth forever. This is my conclusion.

In the Chapter 5, I would like to present the way of human life to adapt themselves to nature, or the third way of life.

Chapter 5 The Third Way of Life

1. Unified Awareness

The third way of life is to live adapting ourselves to nature with the brain, or wisdom. To obtain this wisdom, we need to obtain unified awareness, and try to systemize social science under this unified awareness. Then, first, I will clarify the unified awareness that would be the foundation of systemized social science. That will be a unified form of principle awareness I have been presenting so far. I will try as much as I can.

In writing or speaking, the opening part is the most important. If the opening part does not go well, oftentimes the story ends without any impressive part on the way. There are desired ways to start in anything. The same can be said for how to think about matters. When we think about complicated civilized society, we can start by any part of it and continue satisfactorily, but most of the time, that reaches a deadlock. However, there is one way of starting that does not reach the deadlock. That is the way of starting with thinking about the existence of humans. I have been thinking for 24 years, and I am confident to say this: people say that the truth is only one, and I believe this is it.

Then, why doesn't the thinking way of starting with the existence of humans reach a deadlock? That is because humans are the root of everything. To state more concretely, in societies primitive or civilized, or in problems related to air, water, food, population, scientific technology, cities, transportation, or prices, or in philosophy of Jesus Christ, Marx, Keynes, nothing is unrelated to human existence. To state reversely, if humans do not exist in this world, no problem involving humans would not have occurred, and all the problems have occurred because humans exist. Humans are the root of everything, and the way of thinking starting with the root element does not reach a deadlock. However, that should be understanding humans at their fundamental level as they are. I would like to discuss in a concrete manner.

We were not born into this world with our own will. However, by any coincidence or situations, since the moment we were born, with our instinct of maintaining the self, we start making our efforts in letting ourselves survive without reasoning. This is of course the same for animals in general, not only humans. While some of them require parents' help or protection while they are young, animals have to repeat themselves by taking in food, air, and water from the environment, and putting out waste to the environment.

Here is the circulation of substances. The fact that humans exist on earth means circulation of substances is occurring around humans. This is the economic activity. This economic activity gets bigger or needed when many humans with physiological desires, or population, exist. Therefore, according to the size of the population and economic activities, society has expanded.

To this basic economic activity, the secondary and tertiary sectors are added by diversified desires, inventions, and discoveries of humans, and further, arts, culture, communications, and transportation joined, making today's diversified society. In this way, starting with considering the root of human existence will give you a clear understanding of everything without reaching a deadlock. Also, if you understand the universal logic lying at the bottom of all activities of humans as "the logic of expanding circulation of population, food, and brain", conveniently and curiously enough, you can explain all human activities.

In other words, if you understand logic and think based on it, you can understand all problems in society one after another. I have been able to discuss various problems on the past way of human life based on this logic, and I am confident that I can discuss various matters concerning the future way of human life based on this logic.

Now I would like to explain "the logic of expanding circulation of population, food, and brain".

In Chapter 4 "The Commonality of the First and Second Ways of Life", I explained about the logic of expanding circulation of population, food, and brain that this logic controls humans consistently in the primitive and civilized times as well as in the future, or as long as humans exist. What caused the population to prosper in the primitive era increasing to the full capacity of the earth to its limit and what made humans break through the deadlock toward civilization was this logic. What caused civilization to prosper, as reaching the second deadlock is also this logic. I believe there is nothing that cannot be explained with this logic. Of course it is possible for us to discover the reason for today's deadlock, how to solve problems, and the new way of life with this logic, because it is the root logic of everything in society.

The logic of expanding circulation of population, food, and brain

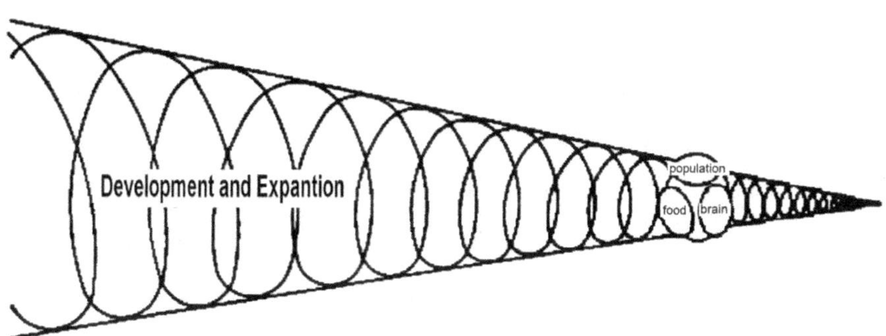

I would like to explain clearly. To begin with, humans exist. They have desires to eat and have sex, and have a brain. To survive, they consume food, and when they grow up they satisfy the desire to have sex and generate offspring. This is how human population increases. Brain plays the role of eliminating obstacles in the process. With this same logic, humans have developed while expanding as shown in the above chart in the past 20,000 years on the finite earth. During that time, they reached the first deadlock, but broke through after struggles. However, today, at the second deadlock, it is difficult to tell they can break it through. However, if they understand this universal logic exists in society and learn from it the direction of society and how to manage it, it can be possible to break through the second deadlock. I would like to explain concretely.

Today's society has become a giant, complicated, and incomprehensive society. However, everything has essence, or basic. If we understand the basic from the view of occurrence and understand the logic, we should be able to clarify the complete picture of society accurately.

Nature gives life to humans and at the same time sets conditions to survive. On the other hand, the humans who are given life are not born or live with purpose, but they live supported by their instinct to survive without reasoning. More precisely, they have the desires to live and to eat to live, and take actions to nature. This takes the form of population and food, or economic activities. From the instinct of preserving the species, population always tends to increase, and food is required to be secured to feed the population, requiring economic activities to expand in circulation. This relationship is common both to the primitive society of 2 million years ago and today's society, and the future society of tens of thousands of years ahead. It is the principle that will never change as long as humans exist.

Let's look back on history. As the economic system shifted from collecting from nature to cultivation and rearing, social system shifted from primitive society to civilized society, changing greatly in quality. However, have these changed the essential relationship between nature and humans, and the principle of human life? The life under the natural economy, the life was natural, as people had to depend on natural law and the environment to survive. On the contrary, under the economy of productive and rearing, life is productive by cultivating plants and rearing livestock animals. Indeed, there seems to be a big difference between the two lifestyles, but cultivating and rearing are the application of a few percentages of natural law. In other words, it is just that humans give support to the natural growth force to make it efficient. Therefore, the change of the economic system does not mean a change of essential relationship between nature and humans.

Also, the change of economic system does not mean that humans can live without eating food nor population increase has stopped. Humans' principle of survival has not changed at all. When we say there has been a great change in quality with the shift from the primitive era to the civilized era, we tend to think that the basic way of life has also changed, but since 2 million years ago when humans appeared to any form of society in the future, the principle that humans live on this earth, eat food from nature, and bear children, will never change. In this sense, the life of simple economic activity in the primitive era that lasted 1.99 billion years is the very model way of life. It is the basic form of economic activity and life that develops their complicacy forever.

This basic economic activity and the way of life lie at the root of the ever-lasting society, the chassis of a vehicle, as its frame. Primitive society is a society of chassis only, and the modern society is a society that is covered with body with decorations. Therefore, modern society does not show the structure or the original form. To sum up the above, however long and complicated human society continues changes, a forever universal logic lies at the bottom, and the society does not change irregularly or unexpectedly.

Therefore, we should stop seeing the branches and leaves of modified and expanded society, or phenomenon of society, but we should have a view to see the essence of society. With this view of essence, we can find the eternal way of life.

The third way of life, the theme of this chapter, is the life in which we stop the increase of population, diversified desires, and industrialization, and then keep balance with food, water, air, space, solar energy, and the ecosystem the earth has to offer. However hard humans try, they cannot create natural law, therefore they cannot go beyond nature. In other words, they cannot change the finite condition of the earth to infinite condition. As humans are of such beings, there is no other way than controlling "the logic of expanding circulation of population, food, and brain" that is seen consistently in the humans' lifestyle of 2 million years, and the logics effective around the logic such as logic of infinity, social self-operation force, and the principle of the stronger prey on the weaker, and live in balance with finite ecosystem of the earth. However, this is the original way of life that can allow humans to stay on the earth forever. In other words, it is the way of life that does not reach a deadlock not like the first and the second way of life.

As mentioned above, we can understand everything about the way of human life unitedly. This understanding can be helpful to humans as general wisdom. However, if we systemize social science based on this unified awareness, the human brain will further become solid and concrete. If this becomes the reality, humans, who have evolved themselves into animals that have to depend on their brain to survive, get on track of true evolution for the first time.

I consider the understanding of earth's ecosystem, social ecosystem, and human ecosystem unitedly not as ideology but the truth, because I did not create but I realized what exists in a form anyone can understand. I am also confident that, in modern times when the lives of 3.9 billion people are in danger, the philosophy genuinely expected to be found is this philosophy. In other words, this logic has been expected as the duplicate logic of natural logic, or the truth that everyone can agree on.

I have tried to unify the principle recognition I have discussed fragmentally in previous chapters up to Chapter 4 under the theme of unified recognition, but they are not satisfying to me. However, I will close this section believing that my wise readers will understand what I have discussed even if I do not unify the fragments perfectly.

2. Society Led by Wisdom

The third society is a society led by wisdom run by the intelligent brain. The study object of social science is society. In Chapter 3, I wrote that "Social science does not develop because society is complicated and difficult to understand. However, if we look closely, there are characteristics in society that can be understood one after another and unitedly. If we earnestly work on it, society can be understood unitedly, and based on this unified understanding, social science can be greatly developed." In the previous section, I described the unified awareness that can be gained one after another. I am going to discuss the systemization of social science based on unified awareness in the next section, but I am sure that the systemized social science will serve as a true and practical human brain to correctly operate future civilized society. Then the third way of life will be necessarily a society led by wisdom. This means that humans will become the ideal forms for the first time after civilization. I have now mentioned "the ideal forms", but as I have repeatedly stated and as everyone feels, humans have to become the ideal forms otherwise there will be no future for humans. Vague knowledge or politics that work after events cannot address the logic of society and nature, and humans will be excluded from natural selection. It is becoming the era when humans will go extinct if we do not bring the brain that is authentic in real sense.

Even at this stage, some people expect politics to help them, but that is a foolish idea. Politics in the lack of a true brain is only agreeing to the society's self-operation. They are only playing the final processing role and leading us to destruction. As I discussed previously, politicians are not responsible for that. Politicians are elected by citizens; therefore they look superior to citizens. However, politicians cannot go beyond the level of citizens, nor conduct politics beyond their level. Politicians who are elected by foolish citizens who do not know how to understand society or how to live in the future are also foolish politicians who can only conduct foolish politics.

That is why there is no help in expecting politics. What we should expect is a brain, or wisdom, that improves the level of the citizens, saves them from destruction, and leads them to an eternal way of life. If the brain is vague, we cannot see our fate nor can we create effective plans or policies. Before we act, planning is needed, and before planning, the brain, or wisdom is necessary. Brain is the strength of humans, and the life of humans. Especially in the future, humans cannot survive without the authentic brain. The lifestyle led by this authentic brain is the expected and desired way of life.

I am now writing about the third way of life, but in the essential sense, the third way of life is not the way we will live from now on. It is the way we have to create by a wise brain, not the way of life we will have. Humans may not be able to shift to the third way of life and become extinct as living the second lifestyle. Therefore, the first prerequisite is to have a wise brain to shift to the third way of life, and also to operate the third society properly after the shift. I will explain the role of politics there. The third society will be a society led by a wise brain. If such a wise brain does not appear, the third society will not be created.

If the fake third way of life is created with our uncompleted brain, that will lead us to destruction. You may think that the fourth or fifth ways of life would be possible after the third way, but the ways after the third way will not be created. There can be a modified way of the third way of life, but that will not be a completely new way beyond the third way. The third way of life is the final and eternal way of life.

Now I would like to discuss the politics of the third society. Politics of the third society will be democratic. However, as citizens will be all wise because of the think-tank (I will explain in the next section), politics of the third society will not be foolish but intelligent. Rather, as the think-tank would have discovered everything in the third society, the direction of country management and how to operate it will be drawn on a blue-print concretely and clearly, therefore politicians will be experts who execute what is written there. In other words, they will be the pilot of the plane or a bullet train where everything is organized. Therefore, the politicians in the third society will not study philosophy like today and they do not need to bear all responsibility to themselves.

On the other hand, however, they will not be able to enjoy their authority or the feeling of superiority. The third society will be practically a society led by wisdom, or a society led by social science, run by the true brain of humans.

3. A Think-Tank

Now we have come to the stage where we should systemize social science and make efforts to gain concrete wisdom for humans. However, it is not enough that planning of systemizing social science is completed as if chemical symbols lined up on paper. The problem is rather how to have the system realized in the actual society, so we have to think from that point of view. The best way for that is to form a thinking factory, or a think-tank, a brainpower, and have them organize it concretely.

As I will go in details later, the third society will be a society that has the elements of planned balance, a global state, planned economy, democracy, liberty and equality, and mixture of races. The think-tank should be formed to be appropriate to realize such a future society and further to manage it. To form such a think-tank, a preparation committee should be formed at first, and it should start with examining the unified awareness and then draw a picture including systemization of social science. For your information, I would like to present my idea of a think-tank.

A human body works as a harmonious body of liver, stomach, eyes, nose, and everything systematically in a coordinated fashion in a rhythmic manner. Each organ is never self-asserted but mutually helpful. A think-tank should be formed in the same manner. Firstly, all the research institutes around the world should form one large think-tank, and each institute should conduct research following the directions by the headquarters in a unified manner. In other words, the think-tank should be formed and operated to allow them to present practical results that comply with the unified recognition.

The headquarters play various roles. Firstly, it should be participated by members of various fields such as philosophers, social scientists, natural scientists, engineers, government administrators, critics, and global citizens, and it bears the role of directing and controlling the large think-tank.

Secondly, the headquarters should be open to the global state and its citizens as a knowledge bank or a reference center, and be able to answer easily to demands for any information. Of course the information can be available through branch organizations.

The third point may include elements above, but the headquarters should know the future way of human life and everything ahead of time and be always prepared to provide all necessary planning, policies, and agenda for politics. In this case, politics will be the loyal executive body of them.

The fourth point is that the headquarters should strive to improve the intelligent level of the global citizens to the same level of the think-tank through education and mass media, and aim to have all the citizens equipped with wisdom. Then they will become wise public, producing wise politics, and humans will be able to earn eternal life on earth by themselves. Most people will become wise only by understanding unified awareness even if they do not understand the details. People will know what is true and what is false. Then the information flood will end and consensus will be reached, ending all wars.

The headquarters will be the brain body that can satisfy all the necessities of humans. This is generally satisfactory. Then, will it be possible to form such a coordinated body? We have to make it possible. It will be very difficult to achieve. However, the third way of life is the way created with brain. Therefore, if humans desire to exist on the earth, it has to be achieved. Anything can be possible when humans are ready to risk their lives and try to do something. This is the very challenge humans should take with all their efforts of their lives.

I wrote this idea in spring of 1969. When I visited the World Expo in the following year of 1970, I felt I saw a concrete model of it. The headquarters of the expo must have had planned and made every effort well in advance, but I was amazed to see how it was well-organized according to their plan with people from countries around the world with different languages and customs. When I saw it, I thought it was what was wanted. I was even more amazed when I visited the event Indonesia. Their theme was "unification in diversity".

Indonesia consists of more than 100 tribes living on 13,000 islands, with a population of 110 million people. They were still trying to unify the country. I thought it was what a World Expo was about, and at the same time, I became confident that a think-tank would be possible.

Another model of a think-tank is the Apollo program. It is said that 300,000 scientists and engineers participated in the program. All of them combined their efforts together toward one aim. For realization of the third society will require millions or more scholars to form one organization. However, different from the Apollo program, it is an activity that has to be realized at any cost. I am sure that what was possible for the Apollo program can be done for the third society similarly aiming for one purpose. If the methodology had not been established, it may have been impossible, but we have the methodology. I am sure that a project participated by a large number of people like in the Apollo program can be possible. This means the third way of life can be realized, which means that the eternal existence of humans can be possible.

I have presented my rough idea above. I would be honored if my idea can be used as a draft. I will further describe the think-tank in the following sections. I would like to emphasize that the staff who will play the main characters in the think-tank should be a group of social scientists.

4. Education and the End of The Information Flood

I have discussed the unified recognition and the think-tank required for realization of the third way of life so far. I would like to discuss the features of the global state as the third society, the actions Japan should take, and at the same time, the problems of information, labor, and leisure in the third society.

Also, I would like to discuss the issues of respecting humans and consensus. Now I would like to start with education.

Today, education is in chaos to the higher level than ever in history. This is caused by the situation where the teachers are not sure how they should teach. In other words, that is because society has become complicated, and education is not independent from politics and economy, so they cannot provide consistent and pure education. How education is conducted has been always discussed. However, under the low awareness of the level where education is seen as vocational training, or personal preparation for working in society, or as development of personality or creativity, discussions cannot go well and correct education cannot be expected.

Education in an essential sense is to teach everything about how to live. As the way to live is associated with society, when society is not well understood, affirmative education cannot be provided. Society in old times was simple, and it was relatively well understood, allowing education to be provided confidently. However, today, society has developed too complicatedly, and it is not well understood. Therefore, thinking makes vicious circles deadlock, so teachers cannot provide education confidently. The importance of education is the same at any time. It is all the more important in today's society, or rather, it is questioned of the quality today.

Education is not the only matter that is questioned. As society that is the foundation of everything is not understood, everything from economy, politics, to civilization is questioned. Therefore, unless the whole society is understood unitedly, everything including education cannot be understood. I have challenged this problem so far. In the last section, I presented my concrete idea and mentioned the education issue. If the think-tank close to my idea is realized, true education can be regained, and the intelligence level of global citizens will be close to the level of the think-tank will produce intelligent global citizens.

In school education, essential aspects of things should be focused on each level of elementary, junior high, high schools and university to create humans who can understand nature and society from their foundation. Education for adults should be given through mass media, which should focus on essential aspects of things. What is lacking in humans is the understanding of essential aspects of things.

If most people understand unified awareness very well and become intelligent, they will not need to listen to detailed information to make judgements, and information floods like what we see today will gradually end. Today's information flood is terrible. As I discussed previously, society itself has become very difficult to understand and people have diversified views, allowing them to find various topics to talk about. In the capitalism era, mass media has been very active because they can earn as much money as they want just by presenting information. Mass media is a presentation theater where various information and ideas are shared, causing an information tsunami. As if drowning in it, humans are searching for information that can be helpful for their life. However, most information found is just junk, only making the vicious cycle more active.

The modern era guarantees freedom of speech, but if the contents are too diversified and unarranged, the general public does not know what to believe. Therefore, traffic control of ideas is most needed now. This will be conducted by the think-tank. When the think-tank is realized, ideas will be controlled. Even if they are not controlled, intelligent people will choose necessary information, so information will be controlled necessarily. Then there will be no information flood, and mass media will release only information that comply with the unified awareness.

5. Consensus

The third society is a society of lifestyle run by consensus. It has been an era of choices so far, and people could choose how to live, like in the society with slavery, feudal system, capitalism, and socialism. To look at them closely, we find diversity in each of them. Take a society with capitalism, there are various systems such as a system with colonies or without colonies, operated only with economy without armaments, a system with planning, a system that prioritizes social welfare, among many others.

Even there were various alternatives, that was within civilized society, and also along with development with expanding circulation by "the logic of expanding circulation of population, food, and brain". Therefore, humans have realized that there is a limit in everything on the earth and they have only one alternative left.

That is the way of life while humans take initiative to closely adapting themselves to the earth. I will omit the explanation for this as I have discussed repeatedly, but as I see many others discussing similar awareness, I think the common awareness has been already established to a great level. This common awareness is the consensus. Without this consensus by all human beings, the third society will not become genuine, because the third society should be created based on the consensus reached by everyone.

Therefore, everyone should share the unified awareness and reach consensus in a genuine sense. Even though I do not discuss this consensus here, phenomenon tells us so. I believe that the consensus will be reached necessarily someday. In other words, everyone will be able to know matters like whether or not population increase is good, what will happen if people show their egoism in overcrowded situations, and whether or not economic growth is a virtue.

However, the awareness in that case would be the awareness of consensus that cannot be reached if the reality does not catch up. Even if such an awareness is reached led by the reality, if it is too late, the situation of the stronger prey on the weaker will prevail further. Therefore, the consensus should be reached in advance. At the stage where alternatives are still available, or when opinions are diversified, consensus should be reached with the unified awareness on what will happen in the future and everyone should work on realization of the third society.

Also, this consensus should be made not pessimistically or in a resigning manner, but positively. To say concretely, it should not be a pessimistic or resigning consensus made because we have no other choice, no growth expected on a small land, but a positive consensus made because we will shift to living with the brain and the lifestyle complying with the earth with our brain from the point of the logic of expanding circulation of population, food, and brain or the logic of finite earth.

This consensus cannot be reached without a higher value, ideals and principles over the value, ideals and principles that people in different countries stick to. When we are reaching the second deadlock, there is no higher value, ideals, and principles than the consensus of winning the eternity of humans by taking initiative to adapt ourselves to the earth. Therefore, I am confident that this consensus can be reached overcoming various positions of people.

6. Respect for Humans

What I would like to say in connection with consensus is about respect for humans. For some time in the future, the population will keep increasing making the society more crowded. The third society to be realized in the future will be a highly dense society. When population is increased, human life and rights tend to be seen lightly. This can happen also in the third society. However, that should not happen in the third society. Therefore I would like to present the theory of respecting humans and obtain consensus.

This theory of respecting humans was completed in my first years of college, and formed the foundation of the philosophy I have presented so far, and has controlled my actions to date.

The history of the universe is infinite, and the size of it is also infinite. In this infinite universe, it is said that there are countless stars that have life like the earth. We were all born on the same tiny planet Earth in the infinite universe only by coincidence. No one of us was born to this moment in history by our own will. After we were born, we learned about ourselves and realized that we are unique existence. We were not born with any purpose, but from the moment we were born, we live based on our fundamental desire to live and not to die. Society is a group of such individuals.

Humans are said to be the lord of creation or the existence to be respected. However, if we look at the background of existence, humans and other animals are exactly the same, and there is no objective reason to see only humans to be worth respecting. Of course the development of the brain or civilization are not the cause of being respected. Humans are completely equal with other animals. The idea that humans are the existence to be respected is an idea no one in the natural world approves. It is only a monologue of humans without objectivity. Therefore, humans cannot be considered to be the existence to be respected essentially. In spite of this fact, humans respect life and the rights of each other.

Here is the ground of this theory.

From the moment of his birth, every human lives based on the fundamental instinct of desire not to die but to live. No one can deny this desire. No one lives alone in this world. A large number of people with this same desire live together.

In other words, society is a group of people wanting to live. Therefore, if you find someone in the group is annoying and harms his life or rights, you will be revenged by him, his family, or the society, and cannot live in peace any more. This principle of retaliation has existed as the principle of nature since the appearance of humans, or organisms. To keep yourself safe, the principle and the best way is that you do not harm the life and rights of others. I believe this is the reason that, in today's society where a large number of people live together, people are respecting each other's life and personality.

We should understand this universal and fundamental principle and be aware that living while respecting each other is the original way of life. Also we should be aware that honoring each other and mutual concessions are the basics of respecting humans. This is the awareness strongly required in the third society. Such a strong awareness of respecting humans should be rooted at the foundation of the third society.

7. A Global State

The process of expansion of civilized society started with a society of hundreds of thousands of small groups sparsely living on the earth, becoming bigger societies by unification of some groups, and further becoming larger societies by more unifications. Civilized society itself does not have any goal to aim for, but with the logic of necessity worked in the civilized society. Along with population increase, civilized society expanded like a snowball. This activity will continue until the world on the earth becomes one society to its limit.

From the point of such principle of necessity, it is natural to think that all societies on earth will practically become one society in the near future, whether by wars or by peaceful means. This necessity has existed since the birth of civilized society; therefore the global unification of society is the fate since the birth of the civilized society. Humans started with one society in ancient times, and today they are going back to one society, which is very interesting. I would like to go into more details.

In the primitive era, tens of thousands of small society groups existed around the world. it is difficult to imagine how they were just from the number. The reason why there were so many society groups is that smaller groups were more convenient to travel searching for food since humans appeared on the African continent 2 million years ago. As population increased, societies were divided and grown in number, and finally they covered the whole earth thinly in tens of thousands of society groups.

However, since the civilized era started, humans began to settle for agriculture, and it is also convenient to form larger societies to block outside enemies and for economy, so they formed the opposite way from the primitive era. Following the principle, the existing tens of thousands of societies were not divided but expanded their population in each society. To supply the societies with increased population, land and labor (slaves) were needed. Stronger societies occupied weaker societies and absorbed them, and expanded in aggregation.

Then, eventually, some small groups gathered to make bigger societies, and again they gathered to make large societies. This process is obvious from the history of each country. Even a country like the United States that did not go through this process took a variant form. Also, former colonies have become independent countries making the number of countries larger, but this is only a temporal phenomenon, not outside of the process of expansion of societies. In this way, societies expand from small to larger and necessarily form like a snowball. This expansion is caused by the principle of necessity, and it continues until the whole world becomes one society. This principle of necessity is "the logic of expanding circulation of population, food, and brain". This has been realized on earth, and the world is heading for aggregation.

Then, are societies formed in this way peaceful and ideal? The answer is no. They are societies where internal conflicts occur and are on the path toward destruction. Global unified society formed just by the logic of expanding circulation of population, food, and brain, will eventually reach a deadlock and invite domestic conflicts. It will only head for destruction and never become a peaceful and ideal society. Many people unconditionally accept the globalization caused by the principle of necessity, and talk about internationalization and globalization. I wonder if they misunderstand that all problems including education, economy and politics can be solved if they are considered in an international view.

Of course, there are many issues that can be solved in an international view. However, it is not correct to see considering in an international view can solve every problem. From the point of the principle of necessity, the world will become one society in a practical sense, and it will have to deal with the same problems that cannot be solved in one country. Therefore, from an essential view, agreeing to globalization unconditionally without having future prospects and trying to solve problems in that direction is wrong.

People today actively talk about globalization. Why is that? Is it because we are in the era of globalization? Why do we internationalize? If we do not know the true meaning of that, we will just agree with globalization unconditionally on the trend as if it is the best way. Under globalization, everything can be done under international cooperation. No war will occur. Eternal peace seems to be possible if we see things only on the surface. However, globalization is gradually realized because such a situation is desired and everyone strives for it, but it is being realized out of necessity. This globalization from necessity are showing aspects on the surface that people want to agree with unconditionally but actually it is heading for the second deadlock essentially.

In other words, to unify the world means that the population fills the world. Population will cover the earth. When population increases, as Pierre Teilhard de Chardin wrote in his book "L'Avenir de l'Homme (The

Future of Humans)", the world will go toward one human society practically by the pressure of population as a result of aggregation overcoming any hardship. The world society formed in this way will never be the ideal society but a society with fate to reach a complete deadlock and destroy itself.

Then, how can the ideal society be realized? The global state should be the third society. It is a society planned and operated by the think-tank. If the think-tank is a perfect organization, the realization is possible. In other words, the think-tank takes initiative to plan the global state with their intelligent brain, and apply the necessity to realize the third society on consensus of the global citizen. The realization of a global state is not impossible if we take time. This is because a strong internal cause of necessity to aggregation by "the logic of expanding circulation of population, food, and brain" for one reason, and because the foundation of consensus is formed with the existence of the United Nations that has spread the idea of global federation for another reason.

Now, what is the ideal global state, or what kind of society is the third society? I can describe the major features of it as a society led by wisdom, a society founded on consensus, a society of equality, a society of freedom. I have already described the first two kinds, so I would like to explain the latter four kinds in the order of A through D.

A. Society That Never Reaches Deadlock (Society in Good Balance with the Earth)

Society that never reaches a deadlock is, different from the first and second societies, a society that never sees the limit. The causes of society reaching a deadlock are increased population, used-up resources, and environmental destruction. Therefore, controlling these causes is the condition of eternity. This is a task of the think-tank, but I would like to discuss here.

Firstly, I would like to discuss controlling population increase. What makes population increase a problem is in food availability. Therefore, population issue can be said as the same as food shortage issues. The first way of life reached a deadlock because the population exceeded availability of food in nature. Today's deadlock is essentially the same. In other words, today's deadlock was caused by a population exceeding the availability of man-made food. However, the issue of environmental destruction is more visible, covering the surface of the food crisis, making the essence of the problem invisible.

Therefore, without controlling this primary cause of deadlock, we cannot overcome today's second deadlock, nor shifting to the third society. Today, population control policy is conducted around the world, but still the population has not decreased but is on the increase. Humans should obtain international consensus as soon as possible, succeed in controlling the population, and start a lifestyle that is in good balance with the finite earth. However, now that humans have come to this stage, they need to depend on the genuine brain of humans that is systematically created under unified awareness. In other words, we have no other choice than depending on a think-tank. Therefore, succeeding in creating a genuine think-tank as soon as possible is the condition to realize a society that never reaches a deadlock.

Secondly, I would like to discuss controlling the amount of resources used. Today's industrialization is supported by various resources from the earth. However, while the resources are finite, industry is only expanding and resources are running out. If resources are used up and industry is decreased, the population that has been supported by industry will rapidly decrease. In the worst scenario, population will decrease to the number that can be sustained by agriculture only. However, if industry decrease, production of agriculture will also decrease. Population that can be sustained by agriculture only will be smaller than we think. To avoid such a situation, we should stop population increase and economic growth, control resources, and shift to the economy circulating around agriculture.

Thirdly, I would like to discuss controlling environmental destruction. As we looked at the characteristics of nature in the previous chapter, the natural environment has the characteristic of changing to the negative direction to be inconvenient to humans. Development of civilization is the process of creating a human environment in natural environment and insert it into natural environment. Therefore, civilization is creating a negative environment that is inconvenient to humans. This is deeply related to population increase and growth of industry as I explained previously. Therefore, we should prevent these growth and limit the change of the natural environment within the capacity of humans' internal environment. I discussed these subjects previously, so I am not going deeper on them, but in any case, we can realize society that keeps a good balance with the finite nature and never reaches a deadlock only when humans take initiative to adapt themselves to nature with their wisdom.

B. Peaceful Society Without Wars

Wars are the most hated matters to humans, but the causes were always created under the principle of aggregation (expansion to re-organization caused by the pressure of population) in civilized society out of necessity. To say more concretely, each society after civilization increased population under the principle of aggregation, and along the increase, it tended to be unified with another over any obstacles. When that happened, when awareness was low and prejudice, strong egoism, and exclusiveness were strong, a war occurred, and if the situation was the opposite, unification was achieved peacefully. Most of the time so far, expansion was made by wars because awareness was low and exclusiveness was strong. The principle of aggregation continues until the whole world is unified, therefore the possibility of expansion by wars will continue. However, we should avoid wars at any cost and try to achieve globalization with the strong will of humans. There are two reasons why I emphasize this.

The first reason is the destructive power of today's weapons. The total amount of nuclear weapons owned by countries around the world is said to be the amount that can destroy humans twice or three times. Therefore, if a world war occurs involving nuclear weapons, humans will end, far from aggregation. No one will be the winner. There is a Japanese saying that goes "Everything is meaningless without life". We should avoid such wars and engage in peaceful negotiations. If we are ready to take such a risk, anything can be possible with the spirit of mutual respect in the first place. Globalization should be realized not by wars but with peaceful means. This is the first reason.

The second reason is that the global state will have no meaning if it is formed too late. As I wrote previously, the world will be practically unified even if we leave it alone. Apart from whether that is by wars or with peaceful means, it will be unified by the principle of necessary aggregation, the essence of which is the logic of expanding circulation of population, food, and the brain. The established society will always have many internal conflicts, and will reach a deadlock in various aspects, and will destroy itself in the end. Therefore, to avoid such a situation, we should change our today's way of life in which we just adapt ourselves to the logic of necessity to the way in which we take initiative in applying the logic of necessity and with humans' will to build a global state with peaceful means in advance. This is the second reason we should realize globalization while avoiding wars and by our own will.

The global state, or the third society is a society which should be realized by the think-tank. Therefore, what I have stated is the subject that the think-tank should address. The global state should be operated by the think-tank in a peaceful manner as a police state that controls all possible causes of internal conflicts.

C. Equal Society

To keep people in good relationship with each other in the global state, everything has to be equal. Even if global citizens are generous and connected with each other on consensus, the time will come when they cannot bear it if they are not equal. Therefore, the prerequisite for the global state is equality. The global state will be organized like the United States of America. The possible issues will be adjustments of difference in sizes of each state that is currently a country, density of population, food production ability, resource availability, economic power, race mixture, among others. I believe that these can be solved as domestic issues under the awareness of the community with common destiny, because they are connected with consensus that the global state solves problems and humans cannot survive in the future without the global state.

Generally speaking, today's differences in land size, amount of available resources, economic power and many other elements occurred by coincidence, or out of principle of first comer first winner or the stronger prey on the weaker. The global state will re-organize and re-systemize these elements on consensus for the survival of humans, so there is no chance that consensus cannot be reached. Of course, it will take a considerably long time for a perfect equality, but it has to be realized on consensus reached by discussion however long it takes. However, before it is too late, control of global population increase and expansion of human desires should be addressed as priority. I will discuss this issue later in the section of Japan and the world, so I will stop here.

D. Free Society

Being free means to be able to act on your own will without being intervened by anyone, and this is what everyone desires for. The ideal way of human life is said to be the same; being free and all desires are fulfilled. However, freedom is not infinite but there is a fixed amount shared by everyone. If population increases, the share becomes smaller, and you cannot live as you wish. Therefore, if you try to live a free and ideal life according to your mind in today's density, high level of techniques are required. The techniques here are planning, adjustment, and systemization. In a dense society without a proper planning suitable for it, you cannot live a free and ideal life, or rather, the society itself may reach a deadlock.

Today's society is a highly planned society in a complicated way by many legal laws and systems. Today's level of freedom is guaranteed because the society is planned and well organized. A major example is the traffic issue. Increasing the number of vehicles, paving roads, and establishing traffic rules are all trying to catch up with each other, but it is a successful example. All issues in society should be conducted with planning like traffic issue. However, not all issues are successful like traffic. Most issues are not fundamentally addressed under a unified planning, but only treated after problems occur. Overall, society is very complicated.

The global state has to be a society with complete planning presented by the think-tank. That society should be well-coordinated in density, with more space and freedom. Of course, the global state is a society created on consensus of the global citizens. It is a society where no one is bound by ideology or anything. (The global state is a society based on unified awareness without ideology.)

In other words, while the earth is stable, population has increased endlessly causing civilization more complicated. Therefore, if we do not create an organized social order, the citizens will not feel the purpose of life not to mention freedom in the society. It is a planned society presented by the think-tank that answers people's concerns about losing their freedom if fundamental measures are not carried out seriously. That is the global state.

To be freer in a dense society, we need thorough planning, coordination, and systemization. As the density grows further, planning, coordination, and systemization will mean the same as freedom.

8. Labor and Leisure

Humans' desires are diversified and infinite. Industrialized society can make human desires infinite by the chain of desires and purposes. If human desires become endless, factories built everywhere around the world would never be enough. Today's society is in this tendency. This economic tendency is supported by the idea that business and labor are good. Enterprises keep expanding their organization with the purpose of seeking profits only, producing luxurious or low-value items, selling them with advertisements, and demanding more population growth for more labor force.

Workers also believe labor is virtue, unconditionally accept the system of "If you won't work you shan't eat", simply believe that companies that pay well are good even if they produce low-value products, and work without complaining. Of course this economic logic occurred with "the logic of expanding circulation of population, food, and brain" at its foundation, but going along with this economic logic will naturally lead to destroying the earth's ecosystem and the environment as a whole.

Destruction of the environment has become today's big issue. Reconsidering thoughtlessly endless production, shortening operation hours, or shift to five-day workweek have started to be seen. As the idea that productions should be conducted within the earth's ecosystem in a circulation manner is accepted widely, operation hours will be further shortened, and four-day or three-day workweek will be applied in the future, otherwise we cannot sustain the economy within the earth's ecosystem forever.

The third society is a society of lifestyle that respects the ability of the finite earth. Economy operated there will be a circulating economy with almost no growth. Therefore, the society should adapt a four-day or three-day workweek. When that happens, the notion of "labor is virtue" should be abandoned, and the better lifestyle is to have 20 or 30% specialists work, and the life of 70 or 80% normal people should be supported by the global state and enjoy their hobbies. The economy of the global state is operated by the state, so this should be possible if that is wanted. In such a society, no unemployment problem will occur and everyone will be happy if not wealthy. The other 20% of labors, farmers, scientists, and politicians should work with some kind of special treatment or by taking turns.

(You may find it surprising to see the number of 70 or 80% of free people, or jobless people, but when you consider that 50% of the population today are jobless, so this is not surprising. Jobless people today are children who are high school students and lower, college and university students, post-graduate students, over half of housewives, elderly people, most sick people, wealthy people not needing to work, unemployed people, and others. 70 or 80% of free people are little more than the total number of these people.)

The third society is a society that adjusts itself to the ability of the finite earth, and its economy is a circulating economy with hardly no growth. Therefore, the third society is where population and desires are controlled on consensus, and global state enterprises do not harm the earth, not aiming to expand, labors are 20 to 30% of the population as explained above, and most people are free people whose living costs are supported by the state growing vegetables for themselves.

School education for most students except special students should be only mandatory education, with focus on essential issues to teach how to live on the earth as humans of the earth.

Studying for education should not occur and competitions of school entrance examinations will not occur. Education fees should be free and the society is in a relaxed atmosphere. Otherwise humans cannot stay on earth forever.

Future humans should consider various matters such as the relationship between the earth and humans, why they were born, if it is to work or to play. It may seem to be a difficult task, but they have the fundamental thinking method, so they do not need to consider it as a difficult task.

Now let's look at future leisure.

People today seem to think that leisure is to spend money actively on holidays, but I wonder if this is right. People who never play or have never had leisure time are treated as if they do not have their own identity and are controlled by the leisure industry telling them how to spend their free time. Leisure is having time for yourself free from work, and nothing to do with the leisure industry. It should be spent as people desire. Following campaigns by the leisure industry and making yourself busy with their programs is not the right way to spend your leisure time. You can join such programs sometimes but you cannot always join them throughout your life. In the third society where most people will be 100% free, they should not join such programs.

Leisure in the third society should be spent to satisfy inner happiness, such as arts including literature, poems, music, calligraphy, painting, scientific studies, or sports. Today, some people say that working is a human instinct and you can obtain the joy of life only through working, but I do not follow this idea. Humans are not born to work. I believe playing is the essence of humans. I think people in ancient times spent time playing. In the third society of the global state, playing that does not cost money should be developed within the circulating economy so that humans can spend time without feeling boredom. The lifestyle of people in the third society should put priority to living while maintaining orders in the natural ecosystem.

9. Japan and the World

The central value in and after the Meiji era of Japan was to catch up and go ahead of other countries. Before World War II, the United Kingdom and France were the goal, and the U.S. became the goal after the war. Japan should have been satisfied to have caught up with them, but on the contrary, Japan lost its goal and went into confusion. In this sense, it is similar to the U.S.

The United States of America, once a pre-developed country, became a giant country by setting its goal to Europe, but they are in confusion after catching up with Europe. Japan has become a country that has to be the first one to step on a path no other country has ever stepped on. Other countries around the world can refer to Japan's trials and errors to make their decisions for their own development, but what should Japan follow as their standard? This has become a big issue.

However, there is no need to worry about that, because in the future, Japan only has to act based on the unified awareness as I have discussed. To say concretely, Japan should recognize "the logic of expanding circulation of population, food, and brain" and "the logic of aggregation", and create the world order, or rather, the global state, to comply with earth's ecosystem. This path will comply with any principles and all problems can be solved in the process. This is the only path Japan should choose, and it should take the direction for the sake of all humans around the world.

In August 1945, Japan was defeated in World War II, forcing 80 million people to live on 4 islands of total area of 370,000 square kilometers. Japan had already lacked resources and food before the war, and it started the war to solve this problem, but ironic enough, it lost the war and had to go through the experience of heavy overpopulation. The only path left for Japan was the processing trade. Fortunately, Japan lost the war but it had mountains and rivers. It had water to generate electricity. Therefore, it stopped river flows, generated electric power, processed imported resources into products, exported them, imported food with the profit, and it could feed the nation. Since that time, Japan became a country that cannot survive without good relationships with other countries, but in reality, with such relationships, it made growth with trading and became the third largest economic country.

There were also other fortunate incidents. Japan fought in the imperialistic war to solve the problems of population and resources, but it was defeated and could not solve the problems. However, after the war, the world shifted to the economic system that can be sustained without having colonies, and Japan obtained the chance to develop. What could not be realized by the war was realized easily by the change of the world economic system after the war. It was only fortunate. If the world had maintained imperialism, Japan would not have gone above the fourth-level country. The growth of today's Japanese economy was supported by some fortunate factors. The basics of them were the small land, limited resources, and manpower of 80 million people locked in the country with limited amount of food. In other words, it was the desires and strong attachment to the lives of 80millions of people. This continues to date.

Herein lies the reason for Japan becoming an advanced country led by great economic development and at the same time the leading country in pollution. Pollution means destruction of the environment. As I have discussed earlier, environmental destruction occurs along with the development of civilization and economy. Advancement of Japan also leads to advancement in pollution. Japan is a processing trade country; it made a great economic development by industrializing its small land. Here lies the reason why it also became the leading country in pollution. In other words, advancement in the economy and population share the same root.

At the writing of this book, Japan has 110 million people on the same size of land when it had only 80 million people, the term "overpopulation" is hardly heard. Why is that? This is because of the processing trade. To see from a different angle, it has expanded the land in a practical sense. The land of Japan remains the same in size and most of the 110 million people reside there. However, they import most agricultural products and industrial resources from other countries. Therefore, in a practical sense, Japan is not a land of 370,000 square kilometers but the same as the size of more than one million square kilometers. This is why we do not feel it is overpopulated, thanks to the change of the global economic system after the war.

However, this has been supported by using land and resources of other countries, therefore it is unstable. If overpopulation or other events happen in those countries making Japan inaccessible to them, 110 million people on 370,000 square kilometers of land are forced to conduct a self-sufficient economy. If this happens in reality, Japan would be the most overpopulated country and the first country to go into destruction in the world. To avoid such a situation, it is necessary to reduce Japan's population and at the same time to self-supply food. When this happens, not only Japan but many other countries around the world would be in a similar situation. However, there would be some countries that can still feed the nation. Out of necessity, another world war would occur. In that case, there would be no happy country any more.

As we can imagine such possibilities, we should create one global organization that is immortally forever now, and Japan should be the leader in creating this global state. In other words, Japan would not be able to solve its problems by trying to solve only its own problems, and in the same manner, other countries would not be able to solve their problems by trying to solve only their own problems. Therefore, following the principle of aggregation, humans should create a global state that cannot be destroyed forever and live happily together, and Japan should be the leading country to actively promote the global state.

If Japan takes the leading position to create the global state after falling into crisis, other countries will suspect Japan's true intention and will not listen to Japan. It would be impossible at that stage to create the global state. Therefore, the earlier the better. We should start immediately.

The order of the process should begin with further examination of the unified awareness, and based on that, a think-tank should be organized, equip the global citizens with wisdom, and then create a global state like a federal state that keeps balance with the earth. I would like to repeat that Japan should take the initiative to lead the foundation of the global state that complies with the earth's ecosystem. Of course, every country should participate in this creation of a global state.

Afterword
("Theory of Eternalization of Human Race")

I have thought as follows.

In the modern, confused society in crisis, if you are genuinely worried about humans and wish to improve the society seriously, even this may sound paradox, what you should do is not to become a big politician, not to become a scholar to work on educating people, not to lead a protest to demand the government for improvement, nor to become a religious leader to change people. Making actions without much consideration will only lead the society to more confusion. It may take some time, but you should understand clearly the currently most needed principle of unification of nature, society and humans, and then present the principle to humans. This is the most important matter.

This may seem to be a negative attitude, but I am confident that this is actually a very positive attitude. This is the way of making haste slowly. I have never intervened in politics, academic studies, and other fields, but I have devoted myself into thinking about the relationship among nature, society, and humans. Finally I have succeeded in compiling my thoughts into this book. The principles written in this book will be the guideline for not only today's people but also for humans in all times in the future.

With this as a turning point, I would like to break silence and become active. Firstly, I will work on promoting these principles, and act like a midwife for the birth of the future of humans. If you agree to my ideas in this book, I would like you to make these principles known widely. Please join me to actively form the correct global opinion.

The future can be destructive or eternal depending on what we do. The key is the actions of ourselves. We should all act with that in mind. I would like to make our future eternal, and for that purpose, I hope to make my best efforts.

Q&As to Make Issues Clear

So far I have presented the whole book of "Theory of Eternalization of Human Race" I published in 1975. Before presenting it, I read it again and again. I was so amazed at its perfection I achieved 46 years ago.

However, after 46 years since I wrote it, the world population expanded from 3.9 billion in 1975 when I wrote it to 8 billion, drastically increasing by 80%, causing global warming, climate change, desertification, water shortage, food shortage, and riots. Population is rapidly increasing even further. Humans will not be able to avoid destroying themselves. I wrote the philosophical book "Theory of Eternalization of Human Race" 46 years ago for avoiding crisis and seeking eternity of humans, but the principles and proposals I presented there have not been used. I am very sorry to see the reality where humans are still conducting politics addressing problems after occurrence with trial and errors in a traditional way and have difficulties.

Therefore, in the last part of this new edition, I would like to clarify the problems in the form of questions and answers so that this "Theory of Eternalization of Human Race" will spread as soon as possible to become the shared awareness and help humans live eternally on this earth.

Q1. What was the most important proposal that was not used?
A1. The proposal presented in the "Japan and the World", such as;

"The central value in and after the Meiji era of Japan was to catch up and go ahead of other countries. Before World War II, the United Kingdom and France were the goal, and the U.S. became the goal after the war. Japan should have been satisfied to have caught up with them, but on the contrary, Japan lost its goal and went into confusion. (snip) what should Japan follow as their standard? This has become a big issue."

"However, there is no need to worry about that, because in the future, Japan only has to act based on the unified awareness as I have discussed. To say concretely, Japan should recognize "the logic of expanding circulation of population, food, and brain" and "the logic of aggregation", and create the world order, or rather, the global state, to comply with earth's ecosystem. This path will comply with any principles and all problems can be solved in the process. This is the only path Japan should choose, and it should take the direction for the sake of all humans around the world."

"As we can imagine such possibilities, we should create one global organization that is immortal forever now, and Japan should be the leader in creating this global state. In other words, Japan would not be able to solve its problems by trying to solve only its own problems, and in the same manner, other countries would not be able to solve their problems by trying to solve only their own problems. Therefore, following the principle of aggregation, humans should create a global state that cannot be destroyed forever and live happily together, and Japan should be the leading country to actively promote the global state."

These proposals were agreed by many readers at that time, but had not much reactions from mass media and politicians. The proposals were eventually forgotten and have never been used to date. Because of that, humans have stopped thinking, causing Japanese politics to practice trials and errors, addressing issues after occurrence, while the politics in other countries are in a similar state. The whole humans cannot think any more.

Q2. Why is population a big issue? How can it be solved?
A2. It can be solved by making the earth one global state.

Population issue and the global state
How far can humans go? The view of "the earth and population" is important.

The earth is a planet floating in space. In other words, the earth we live on is Spaceship Earth, and we are the crew sharing the same fate. Now humans have increased too much, causing excessive economic activities. The problem is until we can be on board this spaceship safely. I have already found the principle to explain this problem clearly, but unfortunately, it is not spread to the public. I have kept saying that you can clarify the problem if you have the view that "population is the main body of the society."

Among the countries worldwide, the major problem of Japan is its declining birth rate, while the world population is the overwhelming number of 8 billion. This is the largest number in 2 million years of human history, and it keeps increasing by 100 million to 200 million people a year on this earth. How long can humans live on earth under the conditions of this muddy-stream-like rapid increase multiplying 35 to 40 years and the economic activities that satisfy their desires? Humans should see the circumstances from this point and take countermeasures immediately, otherwise they will find themselves in crisis. I would like to present my theory I have gained through my 70 years of thinking and shared in my books and website.

Where and when did humans appear and how did they live?

Humans appeared after evolving from monkeys in one corner of Africa 4.5 to 4.6 billion years of the 9 billion lifespan of the earth, which was 2 million years ago. They hunted and collected food from nature like other animals. However, as they had evolved the brain and they were wise, they could use natural law to live, and increased their population more than other animals did. The increased population found it more convenient to form small groups of society to hunt and collect food. As the population in one society grew bigger, they divided the society into smaller groups like honey bees do. Repeating this process of dividing groups, small societies covered the whole world thinly. This era lasted 1.99 million years, and the population grew to be one million. When humans saw the limit of this lifestyle, they started agriculture and farming applying natural law, and produced food. Agriculture needed various tools and settlement. They started to make larger groups of society and settled in one place, the opposite lifestyle from the previous life. After they settled and made a larger society, they needed rules and a military to protect themselves, as well as development of weapons. More food availability allowed them to increase their population, which urged agricultural civilization. Further increased population formed big cities and then formed a country. The civilization developed into ancient times and to the middle ages. In the 18th to 19th century, The Industrial Revolution occurred in the United Kingdom and other countries, which made industry successful to date.

We have to pay attention to the fact that the population increased only one million in 1.99 billion years since the appearance of humans on Spaceship Earth, but after agriculture was started, it increased to 8 billion people in only 10,000 years. For 1.99 billion years, only 0.5 person a year was added to the population, but now 100 million to 200 million people are added every year. We will have more friends, but cannot just welcome this rapid increase. If this increase continues, it is expected to reach 1.5 billion to 5 billion in the next 10 years, and 15 billion by the middle of this century.

It would be great if a larger population would bring us happiness, but the reality is the opposite. Dense population on this small earth will urge natural selection forces to eliminate humans. Humans can develop scientific technology, but they cannot make the earth bigger nor create natural law. They can just use the natural law to survive.

We need the awareness that population is the main body of society

We need to pay extra attention to another aspect of population which we have considered just one of many social issues. That is the awareness that population is the main body of society. Without humans or population, society does not exist, and no one needs to worry about anything. We should be aware that the fundamental cause of social problems is population, and we seriously consider how to stop population from increasing. We cannot eliminate overpopulated humans like koala bears or monkeys. The whole world should work together to control the population. With issues like global warming, environmental contamination, resource shortage, food shortage, destruction of ecosystems, among others, the Spaceship Earth has reached its limit for humans to coexist. More crew members will increase the number of populations changing the earth's environment and strengthen the natural selection force, then humans will all fall down at the same time. This problem has become visible to anyone, and it will be more terror than the novel coronavirus pandemic.

Humans cannot survive without forming the Global State

In my book "Theory of Eternalization of Human Race" I wrote 46 years ago, when the world population was 3.9 billion, I made some proposals. I would like to reemphasis them now. The global politics are conducted with priority to national benefit of respective countries even at this stage. Now humans should create a global state operated with one unified mindset of coexisting on the earth, limit the population to 10 billion or below, and control human desires to let humans survive. If social scientists and politicians start to have the awareness that population is the main body of society and see the human history of 2 million years as one flow from the appearance of humans in a grand historical view, they will see everything and can also predict a distant future. Then they can grow out of divided ideologies and the thinking way of trials and errors as if they are awakened, and they can plan a global state.

It is not the time humans are discussing religions or territories any more. Lands were not owned by anyone until 10,000 years ago. When a global state is formed, lands will be owned by everyone. Humans should eliminate the time bomb of population and desires immediately, and open the path to live together with the earth. For that purpose, the politics should not be symptomatic treatments but solving all problems from the fundamental cause. The plan should be written by a group of social scientists. We have far less time than it looks. If it is a cancer, you have only one or half a year left to live. It is an urgent issue for all human beings living on the earth.

Q3. What was the cause of the fall of ancient civilizations?

A3. Overpopulation was the common cause.

All ancient civilizations such as Roman, Mesopotamian, Egyptian, Greek, and Inka in South America, are said to have fallen in the end due to overpopulation that caused desertification of surrounding lands and food or water shortage. Fall of civilization in ancient times was an event that occurred in one corner of the world, but now the world has become one area. If humans repeat following the same fate, we should be aware that a fall in our times will lead to the extinction the of all humans. And the time has already come.

The world population is speeding up its increase endlessly on this earth of limited capacity. Comparing it to rain, if we do not stop the downpour of population falling harder, the earth will be flooded and will not allow humans to survive.

Since humans appeared;

Population of 10,000 years ago was 1 million, requiring 1.99 billion years

Population of 4,500 years ago was 100 million, requiring 5,500 years

Population of Year 0 was 200 million, requiring 2,500 years to have 100 million more people

Population of 1000 AD was 300 million, requiring 1,000 years to have 100 million more people

Population of 1650 AD was 500 million, requiring 325 years to have 100 million more people

Population of 1800 AD was 1 billion, requiring 30 years to have 100 million more people

Population of 1900 AD was 2 billion, requiring 10 years to have 100 million more people

Population of 1960 AD was 3 billion, requiring 6 years to have 100 million more people
Population of 1974 AD was 4 billion, requiring 1 year and 4 months to have 100 million more people
Population of 1987 AD was 5 billion, requiring 1 year and 3 months to have 100 million more people
Population of 1999 AD was 6 billion, requiring 1 year and 2 months to have 100 million more people
Population of 2040 AD will be 12 billion, requiring 8 months to have 100 million more people
Population of 2050 AD will be 4 billion, requiring 4 months to have 100 million more people

Japanese are the Citizens of the World

If Japanese people continue to care only about themselves in the Japanese society, the pressure of increasing global population and the worsening ecosystem, two major elimination force of the nature, will eliminate them eventually.

It would be an amazing video if the history of humans can be expressed with 10,000 times speed. Even the Japanese people living a careless life would change their way of thinking drastically.

■ Transition of world population

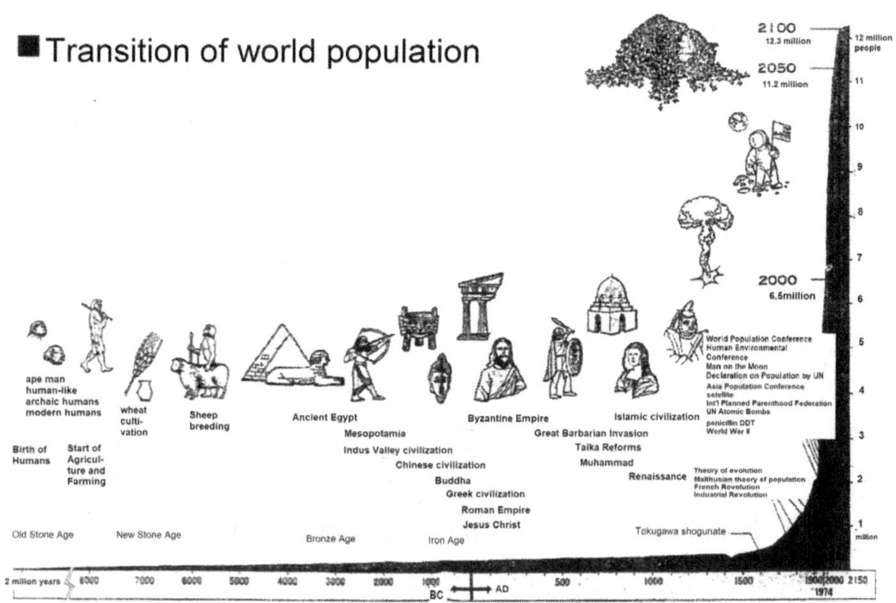

Population Transition of Japan in Recorded History

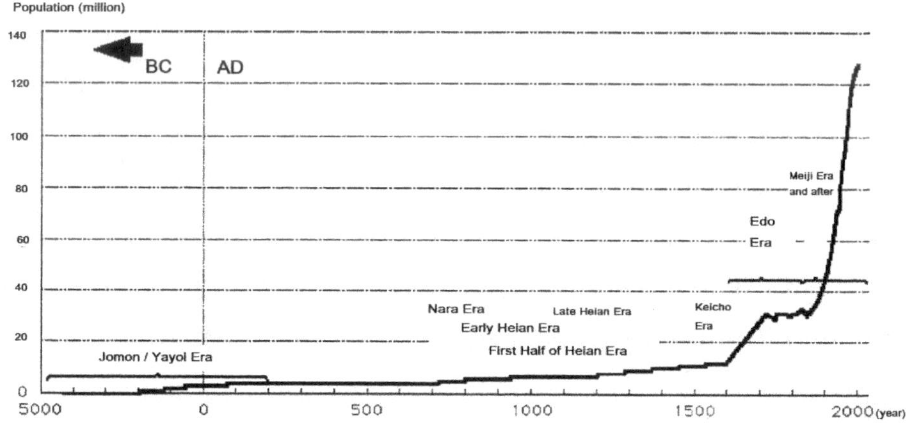

Reference: "Study on Population Decrease and Total National Strength" by National Institute for Research Advancement, "Demographic Data 2004" by National Institute of Population and Social Security Research

Note: "Japanese History from Population (Kodansha, 2000)" by Hiroshi Kito for data in and before 1846, "Analysis of Population Increase (Nippon Hyoron Sha, 1944)" by Yuzo Morita for data between 1847 and 1870, "Population of Japan after Meiji 5" by Statistics Bureau, "National Census" and "Population as of October 1" by Ministry of Internal Affairs and Communications for data between 1872 and 2003.

Q4. Japan has the Minister for Measures for the Declining Birthrate to increase population. Is it appropriate?

A4. Ignorance is bliss. It's a policy to speed up extinction of humans.

Japanese people have very naive awareness about the population. The world population is growing by 100 million a year on this earth of limited capacity. The increasing population generates the energy of desires. (The total amount of energy or elements of global warming one person uses or generates during his 80 years' life in an advanced country is thought to be the amount of energy of one atomic bomb that fell on Hiroshima or Nagasaki. I hope someone can calculate it.) It has become the force of necessity that has spread human society to every corner on the earth, changing the ecosystem to the level humans cannot live.

About the terror of the world population that multiplied just in 35 to 40 years, I wrote in my book 46 years ago as follows. "Population is a devil. It has become the worst terror. It gives us the impression that it is our good friend, but in reality, this devil ruins us gradually. In today's society, atomic and hydrogen bombs, pollution, traffic accidents are the most feared issues, but in the near future, the fear of this population increase will surely be recognized as the worst fearful problem in history." Japan and other countries around the world with the population growing excessively are facing serious problems. Therefore, Japan should have an international view, replace its Minister for Measures for Declining Birthrate to Minister for Controlling Population with a Minister of Forming Global State, and appoint the minister to be the leader of overcoming the human crisis and realization of human eternity.

Here I would like to present "Blog of Prayer on Burning Sand" written by a Japanese who has lived in a foreign country and has been observing Japan from outside.

"Blog of Prayer on Burning Sand" ---- Food Shortage and World Population ----

Since the time I arrived at Narita Airport in the summer of 2006, I have been irritated by the overflooding information.

Among the information, I found the issue of social imbalance caused by the decreasing population due to lower birthrate and aging society, which is causing a decline in productivity and a crisis in tax revenue, as well as a decline in the quality of social welfare. Out of the sense of crisis, Japan has taken measures against childbirth decline. I did not understand this idea.

It was strange to me that it sounded like a sound argument as a grave crisis that affects the survival of future Japan when politicians emphasize the idea. When you hear them speak about it, it sounded so persuasive that everyone naturally accepts. Therefore, we may not realize the fundamental mistakes of politicians on the measures against childbirth decline

I would like to ask the Japanese government if they are seriously supporting the measures against childbirth decline that they are addressing.

Politicians are not conducting immediate improvement of the food self-sufficiency. It would not be an exaggeration to say that the dullness in their sense is the shame of Japan, because their measure against childbirth decline is made due to Japan's lack of international view. This will put Japanese citizens in a very difficult position in the future.

Genuine measures against childbirth decline should be considered at the level of the whole earth, because in the relationship of population increase and food availability of the earth, if population increases, the world will see a food crisis.

When that time comes, what will be lacking most would be animal protein. Do they know the fact that many countries are conducting studies to secure its supply? There are several research initiatives for artificial meat that will replace American beef, and the most promising study is a Russian study of producing maggots. They are animal protein and excellent in growth speed, quantity, and cost. Future children who are born in the measures against childbirth decline may be cooking and eating maggots for their source of protein.

I once had a discussion on the food situation of the world with my friends from the Academic Society of Japan I used to belong to when I was living in Japan. They said they had eaten maggots. After I returned home from Kyoto, I tried them myself. I cooked them like popcorn and ate them.

They were not tasty, and you would not like to eat if you know they were magots. I couldn't tell or ask my children to each of them.

Considering the food situation of the world as a reality, the world will be depending only on plant-based food in the near future. For example, 10 kg of fish is required to cultivate 1 kg of eels. Vast extent of lands are required to obtain grain or grass to feed livestock to gain meat. For the survival of humans, what can be done would be shifting to vegetarians, more production of food by changing lands to agricultural fields, and stopping population increase.

In this global trend, I did not understand Japan's measures for declining birthrate whose only concern is the future of Japan. It was 7 years ago when a delegation of people in the education field from the Chinese government. We had a companion party over dinner in Tokyo among them and Japanese university professors. I had been active with giving lectures on the environment in New York, South Korea, China, and Japan, and my energy urged me to attend the party, and exchange opinions. I asked them about the one child policy from the point of human rights. Their opinions gave me a strong impression that I remember vividly even now.

"If China starves, the world will also starve. Considering the future of our country and the world, for all humans on the earth, we had to implement the one child policy." When we compare these words by the delegation and the measure against declining childbirth, I feel more than surprising but rather shameful for Japan's lack of international sense. I wonder if it is only me to feel that way.

Population will decline, causing decline in productivity and decline in tax revenue that supports Japanese society. However, there may be many other countermeasures. The world is now in the era where various fields are mixed. We do not need to worry about degradation or destruction of social welfare, because we have politicians. If politicians do not understand such easy logic, they may destroy the country. Superior politicians should be imported from other countries. The measures against declining childbirth is an issue raised from the view of focusing Japan only in the global society.

Japan's measures against declining childbirth should be judged considering the relationship between the country's food self-sufficiency rate and population and food of the international society. The idea of considering only the prosperity and maintenance of the country is an old ideology." This is what the author says. Japanese politicians are narrow sighted and conduct politics that go against the earth, while the citizens are not aware of this fact.

Q5 What awareness should humans have toward the population?

A5. The awareness of "First comes the earth, and then humans" is needed.

In the year 1931 when I was born, the world population was 2.3 billion. In only 89 years, it tripled to 8 billion. The world population has doubled in 35 to 40 years like this, former Prime Minister Yasuo Fukuda declared at Davos Meeting in Switzerland in 2011 that CO2 of the world should be reduced by 50% by 2050. However, it is expected that the population of 2050 will be 15 million, twice larger than today, and will reach 29 billion by 2080. Therefore, any measure drawn on a static picture that does not consider the explosion of population and desires is only a sophistry just like a pie in the sky or scooping water with a basket. When a prime minister declares that confidently, the citizens and mass media tend to accept the declaration, but natural law is not that naive. No matter what a prime minister or anyone declares, an explosion of population and desires will aggressively affect the ecosystem, and make the conditions worse every day.

The fundamental cause of global warming is the fact that the population with diversified desires are explosively increasing by 300,000 persons every day, or by 100 million to 200 million every year on this earth with limited capacity, and the fundamental cause of food, water, and resource shortage, as well as conflicts is this increase of world population. Unless humans form a global state of consensus of the world within 5 to 10 years, control population and desires, and shift to the life adapting themselves to the law of the earth, they will be led around by the natural selection force and will have no power over it. It is not the time for humans to establish countries and seek profit for the respective countries any more. Humans should have unified awareness and understanding toward the earth immediately.

Let's discuss the unified consciousness and awareness of humans.

Let 50 actors who have never met each other before on a large stage and ask them to play without a scenario. They may not show good performance. They may look like bad actors, or even only temporary staff to fill the space. However, if you give them a scenario, they will soon start to play their roles fairly well.

The world population of 8 billion are similar to the actors bewildered on a large stage of the earth. They are not sure where to go. If you give the actors of 8 billion people a scenario, they will be more confident. If I compare this to magnets, humans are like iron sand spread on a glass board of the earth, each facing different directions. As if you stroke the earth with a big magnet, the consciousness and awareness of 8 billion people will face the same direction as iron sand. Therefore, what is most needed for today's humans is the scenario or magnetic theory that unify the consciousness and awareness of humans. The theory is explained in the "Theory of Eternalization of Human Race". All humans should share the same mindset, change themselves to live with the brain, and try to live eternally on this earth.

For this purpose, humans should stand on the shared consciousness and awareness, urge a group of social scientists who will be the brain of humans that has not appeared yet, let them draw the detailed blueprint of future lifestyle of humans immediately. Based on this blueprint, the global politics that starts from Japan should form a global state and operate the state without making any mistakes.

Q6. What is the process of forming a global state?

A6. Japan should make a scenario and become its leader.

At the very last of "Theory of Eternalization of Human Race", I wrote about the forming a global state as "The order of the process should begin with further examination of the unified awareness, and based on that, a think-tank should be organized, equip the global citizens with wisdom, and then create a global state like a federal state that keeps balance with the earth. I would like to repeat that Japan should take the initiative to lead the foundation of the global state that complies with the earth's ecosystem. After 46 years, the situation has become severer as I had expected. I would like to share the realizable scenario that can be started in Japan.

In today's world, there should be philosophers who play the role of a conductor of a large orchestra to manage human society and a group of social science to play the role of performers. Their absence caused unclear management of human society, and further causing danger of human extinction as a result.

Therefore, philosophers who can explain the fundamental relationship between the earth and humans should appear and write an outline, and a group of social scientists should be organized to write a script to the outline to make it happen. Then, the group of social scientists write the blueprint of human society management and spread it, and then the brains of people around the world will learn the correct way to live and be filled with wisdom.

Such people with wisdom of essence should select wise politicians of the world who will conduct politics considering the earth based on the scenario written by the group of social scientists, and manage the human society without making mistakes.

The philosophy needed for that has been expected among intelligent people in the world to be born in the east, or specifically in Japan. I discovered the philosophy and wrote it in my book "Theory of Eternalization of Human Race" in 1975. As the global intelligent people had predicted, it was born in Japan.

Therefore, firstly Japan should have the strong will to lead the world with this philosophy, and in cooperation with the world, Japan should call on the world to collect excellent social scientific brains to form a group of social scientists and have them draw a blueprint. Japan should become the leader and play the central role to make sure that the politics based on this blueprint can be conducted to allow humans to live on this earth easily forever.

If this is implemented in Japan as its stage, it will be a success even greater than discovering pluripotent cells. However, it is not the time to be excited. Now the fate of humans depends on Japan. Japan should be aware of that and of its responsibility, allocate a budget of one trillion yen for necessary research costs immediately, and call on the world and lead the world to let humans to survive. Hesitation will make everything too late. The ecosystem of the earth has started rejecting humans who do not understand the earth. We should change our attitude so that the earth, our home and mother, will love us, try to understand the feeling of our mother, and adjust our life to the ecosystem.

It is obvious that if Japan consumes its passion on this activity, Japan will revive and can become the world leader, and can also reorganize its turbulent domestic atmosphere.

Q7. What will the system, life, and awareness in the global state be like?

A7. I already explained that in "Theory of Eternalization of Human Race".

The global state will be born out of necessity. In the leading paragraph about the global state in "Theory of Eternalization of Human Race", I wrote as follows. "The process of expansion of civilized society started with a society of hundreds of thousands of small groups sparsely living on the earth, becoming bigger societies by unification of some groups, and further becoming larger societies by more unifications. Civilized society itself does not have any goal to aim for, but with the logic of necessity worked in the civilized society. Along with population increase, civilized society expanded like a snowball. This activity will continue until the world on the earth becomes one society to the limit.

From the point of such principle of necessity, it is natural to think that all societies on earth will practically be one society in the near future, whether due to war or peaceful means. This necessity has existed since the birth of civilized society; therefore the global unification of society is the fate since the birth of the civilized society. Humans started with one society in ancient times, and today they are going back to one society". Now the time has come.

The world population has been increasing to the full capacity of the earth, making the world one society. This is a natural flow, but not an orderly flow nor led by humans with their plan. Like algae fills the pond by eutrophication, humans fill the earth tightly by population explosion caused by sufficiently produced food. It is a global socialization without considering the future.

After the algae fills the pond, it will die out. What will happen to humans who fill the earth? Will they take the same path as algae, or reject fate with a revival strategy? With humans' current ideology of trials and errors, the chance is high that they will follow the same path with algae.

However, a new philosophy has already appeared. If humans change their fate based on it, it is not possible to step out of the algae fate and let them stay on the earth forever.

For that purpose, they have to satisfy some conditions and clear some problems. This means a complete turn from the policies of taking priority on national interest and profits, so it may be difficult to achieve, but under the situation where the relationship between the earth and humans are in crisis, we do not have time left to hesitate; otherwise humans will be selected out from the earth.

We do not have much time to have debates on national interests, capitalism, or maintaining the current systems. All humans should reach a consensus as soon as possible to consider how to survive based on the "Theory of Eternalization of Human Race", a philosophy that appeared miraculously in time. For this purpose, firstly a group of social scientists should draw a blueprint of the society. I would like to present some ideas that will help drawing the plan.

1. "Theory of Eternalization of Human Race" is a fundamental theory that runs through the past, present, and future of human society. This theory should be applied to planning. It is a theory that can freely control population increase or decrease.
2. The way of life in a global state, or the third society, should be a way to live orderly in the natural ecosystem. Humans will not be able to stay on the earth forever unless they choose to live without giving the earth any stress. For that purpose, the current labor society should be changed to a society where people do not work hard, and that should become the common sense of the society.

Humans were not born to work, the same as all other animals. Humans have had to work because of their system, but they should shift to a working habit not stressing the earth as much as possible. Not only the working style but also in playing, the priority is not to give stress to the earth. Ancient civilizations harmed the nature of the earth, and they fell because nature retaliated against them. We should not follow in the wake of their failure.

3. Humans living in the global state should be aware that "Mother earth keeps us alive" and have appreciation toward the earth.
4. For a starter, we should aim to restrain population growth and desires, as well as economic growth, and then reduce them to the level the earth's ecosystem allows human activities to be conducted easily.
5. We should shift from capitalist society that seeks profits to a well-planned society that keeps its balance with the ecosystem. It is a matter of whether humans keep capitalism and become extinct, or create a well-planned society that keeps a good balance with the earth and stays forever.
6. A well-planned balanced society is a sustainable society where humans do not give stress to the earth. It is a society with low-carbon, circulating economic society with almost no growth. It is also a nature-conscious society, and a relaxed society.
7. In that society, 20% to 30% of citizens will work at state-owned production factories, public offices, or financial offices by taking turns receiving special allowances, and majority of others will live being provided for by the state and enjoy their hobbies or working on their home vegetable gardens.
8. The global state will secure the lives of the citizens with the profit from the state-owned product factories and revenues of consumption

tax or others. Neither the state nor the citizens will not spend much money, nor give any stress to the ecosystem. You may say that such a society will be inconvenient, but now that the world population has grown this far, the current amount of freedom should be shared by all people.

9. The global state will provide only compulsory education except for some special people. The education will focus on essential subjects to educate people to be aware of their fate as humans on the earth and to coexist there. There will be almost no school entrance examinations nor competitions for higher education, but the education of the society will be relaxed. Education will be provided for free.
10. In the process of creating the earth-conscious grand design of the global state, the short, middle, and long term detailed strategies can be created.

Q8. What are the problems that can be solved if the global state is established except the population issue?

A8. There are issues of land, nuclear war, food, security, abduction, global warming, and many others.

1. One of the issues that can be solved if the world is united as a global state is the territorial issue. For example, South Korea and Japan have the Takeshima issue between them, and Russia and Japan have the northern territory issue. When the earth is overpopulated and humans are being rejected to stay, it is not the time such issues are disputed. Nationalism has become out of fashion. We should become global nationalists to work together to confront this global crisis. If the world becomes one, the lands are all for everyone. All the lands were not owned by anyone originally until some thousands of years ago.

2. Most wars occur from fear or national interests. If the world becomes one country, such causes will not occur and there will be no need for wars or nuclear weapons. No country possesses nuclear weapons for the safety from itself. In the same manner, if the world becomes one country, nuclear wars will never occur.
3. Food production differs around the world due to the different conditions of land, water, agricultural technology and others, but if the world becomes one country, food production and distribution will become a domestic issue that can be solved in the country.
4. Security of the global state will become possible by reinforcing the police force.
5. Abduction issue of North Korea can be solved if the world becomes one country. It will become a domestic issue and people will be able to visit there freely. The abductees will be able to be reunited with their family members.
6. The major cause of global warming is population. The global state will be formed to solve this population issue. If it is formed before it's too late, the issue can be solved.

My Final Request at the Publication of This Book

I would like to make a request here by referring to the first part of this book "On Issuing the New Version".

In modern times, the principle economic theories and ideas that have influenced the consciousness, actions, policies and economy of humans including the Japanese are "The Wealth of Nations" written by Adam Smith, "An Essay on the Principle of Population" by Thomas Robert Malthus, the economic theories of Max Weber, "Das Kapital" by Karl Marx, the Keynesian Economics, and the Market fundamentalism of Milton Friedman. Other proposals would be "The Limits to Growth" by the Club of Rome, warnings about environmental problems by Lester Russell Brown, warnings of global warming by former U.S. Vice President Al Gore and the IPCC, carbon emission trading suggested by Nicolas Stern, and warnings of human crisis by James Hansen of NASA, among others. However, none of them has come up with theories of how to lead the future generations. Therefore, humans do not know where they should head to and they are directionless, as if they are stray sheep.

This new book "Japan's Direction, The World's Direction" is about the new theory written based on the philosophy made by the brain to directly address to this problem. Therefore, after you read this book, you will clearly understand as if you detangle the knotted thread of the relationship between the earth and humans, as well as human society that has become complicated and has been conducting trials and errors.

Of course, issues such as population, food shortage, global warming, territories, North Korea, wars, education, human mindset, political economy, economic disparity are all covered for the readers to understand how humans should consider and behave on this earth from now on.

I hope many people will read this book, and the theory in this book will be applied widely in education, politics, policies, and various other fields. For future Japan and for the survival of humans, if you are a critic or writer and agree to my theory, please write or talk actively about it. You can copy this whole book, rewrite it in your own words, or in any form.

The power of the general public is even stronger. If you understand my theory, please spread it by words of month. If it will spread from one person to ten, to hundred, thousand, ten thousand, to a hundred thousand, that will change Japan, the world, and humans. Dear readers, please support me.

I would love to have your feedback. Criticism, opinions, or inquiries would be appreciated.

Lastly, I have expressed my world view in a poem. It is not a good poem, but I would like to present it here.

Save Our Mother Earth
Words by Tetsuo Sawada, Visionary Thinker

If you learn the roots, you will see everything
You will see the past, present, and future of humans
Let's all think together
Long time ago, the Earth was born in the universe as a planet of hope
Life was born on the Earth, both you and I are a part of it
Nothing is more precious than life of hope

(repeat) To see smiles on the face of children
Live a life for the future
To Save our mother Earth

The Earth is a tiny spaceship floating in the universe
The only Earth is crying now
We thought we had depended on our wisdom
But there are already 7 billion people
Both you and I are a part of it
Don't make the precious Earth cry
(repeat)

We are comrades on the earth, the crew of spaceship of hope
Embraced by the Earth
Both you and I are life of hope
Let's live happily together
(repeat)

I would like to ask that someone can arrange this poem and set it to a music, and spread it to the world for coexistence of humans.

Bio of Tetsuo Sawada, Visionary Thinker

Born in 1931 in Wakuya-cho, Miyagi Prefecture
Graduated from Tohoku Gakuin University with
a degree in economics
(member of Debate and Social Science Society)
Worked for Nihon Denken Co. (Sendai)
President of Toko Kizai Co. (Sendai)
President of Sawada Research Institute
(Wakuya, Tokyo)
Author of "The Theory of Human Eternalization"
"Japan's Direction, The World's Direction"
"Fireproof Capsule"
"Can you survive?"
Member of the Population Issue Council (Tokyo)
Councilor, Tohoku Gakuin University; President, Wakuya Branch
Candidate for the House of Councilors election (Tokyo electoral district)
twice
Olympic torch runner in June
Loves golf and karaoke (master level)

Author Tetsuo Sawada, Visionary Thinker

Published by - Research Institute, Inc.

8-1 Aza Sengene, Wakuya, Wakuya-cho, Toda-gun, Miyagi, Japan

987-0121

Phone 090-2024-0120

FAX 0229-43-4345

E-mail :sawadasouken1976@gmail.com

Postal Transfer 18130-28279321

www.ingramcontent.com/pod-product-compliance
Lightning Source LLC
LaVergne TN
LVHW010656110826
845149LV00014B/3112

* 9 7 8 0 9 9 1 4 7 8 9 8 9 *